Stranger Than Fiction

Stranger Than Fiction

Vignettes of San Diego History

by Richard W. Crawford

SAN DIEGO
HISTORICAL
SOCIETY

©1995 by the San Diego Historical Society

Printed in the United States of America

Published in 1995 by the San Diego Historical Society
P.O. Box 81825
San Diego, California 92138

Designed by Jill K. Berry

Printed by Crest Offset

Unless otherwise indicated, all photographs in this publication are from the
Photograph Collection of the San Diego Historical Society.

ISBN 0-918740-19-3

The paper used in this publication meets the minimum requirements of American National
Standard for Information Sciences-Permanence of Paper for Printed Library Materials, ANSI
Z39.48-1984. ∞

Contents

Preface

Ten years ago, Kim George, editor of the San Diego Historical Society newsletter, the *History News*, approached me with the suggestion that I provide interesting "filler" material for the newsletter. "Did I have some brief anecdotes at hand, or perhaps stories of strange events or people in San Diego history?" asked Kim. With this prompting I began a series of articles on San Diego's past, published in the *History News* for members of the Historical Society. More stories appeared between 1990 and 1992 in the North County edition of the Los Angeles *Times*. These articles appear here, compiled for the first time in *Stranger Than Fiction*.

I wish to thank several friends and colleagues who have contributed their comments and criticism: Iris Engstrand, Evelyn Kooperman, Patricia McCambridge, Bud McKanna, Ronald Quinn, Joan Taylor; the archives and curatorial staff of the San Diego Historical Society—past and present—Sally West, Larry and Jane Booth, Tom Adema, Cynthia Krimmel, Carol Myers, John McGee, and Barbara Pope; and the book design talents of Jill Berry.

Richard W. Crawford
San Diego Historical Society

The Lost Treasure of Francisco de Ulloa

It happens every six months or so. An eager visitor to the library of the San Diego Historical Society will ask the harried archivists for material on the Spanish galleon *Trinidad*, flagship of explorer Francisco de Ulloa, believed wrecked off the coast of Oceanside in 1540 with millions in Aztec gold.

For centuries the story of the *Trinidad* and the fate of its master, Ulloa, mystified historians. Sailing from Acapulco in July 1539, Ulloa commanded a fleet of three ships: the *Santa Agueda*, the *Santo Tomas*, and the *Trinidad*. Ulloa carried instructions from the conquistador Hernán Cortés to explore the coast to the north and pursue the endless rumors of gold and the legendary Seven Cities of Cibola.

Ulloa found neither. The *Santo Tomas* sank soon after the voyage began. The explorer sailed on, charting the Gulf of California and venturing up the western coast of Baja California. With supplies dwindling, the *Santa Agueda* returned to Mexico. Ulloa decided to continue "with the ship *Trinidad* and these few supplies and men, to go on, if God grant me the weather! as far as I can..."

The *Trinidad* was never heard from again. Lost at sea, wrecked on an unknown coast, or attacked by Indians—for centuries chroniclers had no idea.

In 1952, an Oceanside ophthalmologist, Joseph J. Markey, proclaimed the mystery solved. Using maps and documents uncovered in a Spanish archive, Markey located the skeletal remains of twenty-two white Europeans buried in a cave in the San Luis Rey valley, on the outskirts of Camp Pendleton. The skeletons, along with weapons and gold coins, all dated from the era of the Spanish conquest, according to Dr. Markey.

In a speech before the San Diego Historical Society on January 25, 1952, Markey presented a detailed account of the last days of Francisco Ulloa and his men. Based upon his archaeological evidence and Spanish documents—including a mysterious diary written by a *Trinidad* survivor—Markey described how Ulloa had anchored the galleon in the mouth of the San Luis Rey River on August 21, 1540. Ill with scurvy, most of the crew abandoned the ship and camped

Left: Dr. Markey in a cave in San Luis Rey Valley containing skeletons of 22 Spaniards and three Indians.

Opposite: A field trip to the site of Ulloa's grave. Dr. Markey is kneeling at the far left.

inland near an Indian village by a freshwater lake. Soon the Spaniards, "lacking the immunity built up over the centuries by the Indians," succumbed to dysentery contracted from the polluted waters of the lake. Ulloa himself died on September 5.

Three crewmen from the *Trinidad*, including the diarist, Pablo Salvador Hernandez, escaped by rowing the ship's longboat to Acapulco. Abandoned, the *Trinidad* sank somewhere near Oceanside.

Did Francisco de Ulloa actually arrive in California in 1540, predating Juan Rodríguez Cabrillo by two years? Could the wreck of the *Trinidad* be found, and would it contain, as Markey believed, several million dollars worth of gold?

The public and news media greeted the story with enthusiasm. Trumpeted by Markey, the story reached a wide audience. Less vocal than Markey were a few skeptics. In a letter to the San Diego Historical Society, Balboa Park's Museum of Man curator Spencer L. Rogers, told curator John Davidson that Markey's theories were at "sharp variance with known scientific facts," and warned, "I look with alarm upon the fact that your institution and society would seem to be giving implied support to this gentlemen's theories."

A more specific challenge to Markey's theory came in 1971 from a professor of history, Dr. David Weber of San Diego State University. Weber pointed out that Spanish manuscripts interpreted in the 1930s clearly placed the explorer Ulloa in Mexico one year after his alleged death at San Luis Rey. Spanish court records also show Ulloa testifying in a trial in Valladolid, Spain in 1542.

If Ulloa and the *Trinidad* had returned safely to Mexico, what had Markey actually found in his cave at San Luis Rey? Ralph Heiser, former museum curator

at Mission San Luis Rey suggested the skeletal remains were ape skulls and the gold coins, "common Spanish coins...made of copper and tin."

Markey's manuscript evidence—the Hernandez maps and diary— which he claimed to have discovered in Spanish archives, were unavailable for examination. In response to his critics, the doctor explained that a forthcoming book would include photographs of the documents.

Suspicions of Markey's theory failed to discourage seekers of the lost *Trinidad*. Markey himself ignored the doubters and played treasure hunter. Suggesting that the galleon must have sunk somewhere near the San Luis Rey River, he began launching rafts in the river loaded with tons of scrap iron. By noting where the rafts sank, Markey hoped to locate the logical burial spot of the *Trinidad*. Unfortunately, the rafts foundered erratically in a wide area. After three years of raft building, Markey gave up.

More determined treasure seekers joined the hunt. A group of professional divers called "Aztec Six" searched without success for several months in 1968. The next year, diver Bill Takasato claimed to have found a wreck buried in sand only a few hundred yards from shore. Bad weather and equipment failures forced Takasato to abandon the search.

In 1973 salvagers financed by a Wilmington yacht broker claimed discovery of the wreck. Again, equipment problems were blamed for stopping the work. Treasure hunters were back in 1976. Bill Warren, a nightclub singer and swimming pool salesman, found "a couple of cannons down there" with the aid of a

Dr. Markey with construction workers at his Ulloa digs site

$7,000 metal detector. As late as 1987 Warren was still trying to get adequate financing to continue his quest.

Dr. Markey died in 1985. His promised book documenting the famous Hernandez diary and maps never appeared.

For all the thousands of dollars and immeasurable hours spent searching for the treasure of the *Trinidad*, perhaps the most remarkable fact of all is that Markey's theories have been so widely believed in the first place. An "artfully contrived hoax," concluded curator Ralph Heiser. A hoax, it might be added, that has captivated the public for over four decades.

The People vs. Cave J. Couts

Early Monday morning on February 6, 1865, Colonel Cave Johnson Couts, *(pictured above)* prominent rancher, judge, and politician, from San Luis Rey, stood inside George Tebbetts butcher shop in Old Town. While talking with Tebbetts he noticed a former employee of his, Juan Mendoza, stroll across the plaza and enter the Franklin House.

Minutes later, Couts watched again as Mendoza walked out of Franklin's and into the street. "That man has threatened my life on sight!" he exclaimed as he picked up his double-barreled shotgun and strode out to confront Mendoza.

"Don't shoot him!" Tebbetts yelled, but Couts raised his gun and fired. The shot flew wide and Mendoza ran for his life. From thirty yards away Couts fired again and Mendoza fell, killed instantly by a round of large shot.

The shooting of Juan Mendoza stunned the people of San Diego. Couts was a respected man and popular with the community's elite. But the act of killing an

Old Town San Diego in 1874

unarmed man in broad daylight, in front of several witnesses, could not be ignored.

The local justice of the peace, John Compton, ordered Couts jailed. By Thursday, however, friends had posted $15,000 bail and Couts was released. Months passed, finally in June 1866, the Grand Jury indicted Couts for murder. In October, trial began in District Court.

Testimony revealed what many had known all along: Mendoza was no innocent victim. Weeks before the shooting he had been dismissed by Couts after a dispute over wages. Afterwards, Mendoza swore publicly that he would kill the rancher at the first opportunity. Mendoza's past deeds suggested that the threat was not an idle one.

Forty-six years old at the time of his death, Mendoza had led a violent career, mostly in his native Mexico. As the corrupt alcalde of a mining district in Baja California, he was infamous for extorting money from the population—"particularly Americans." Later, as the leader of a band of revolutionaries, he allegedly murdered nearly a dozen people after robbing them of goods and property.

When it became too hot for Mendoza below the border he came to San Diego, where his wife, "an estimable and useful woman," found employment with Mrs. Couts at Rancho Guajome. Mendoza was hired as Couts' mayordomo.

Trial witness Eugenio Morillo, a long-time acquaintance of Mendoza, recalled that he was a violent man with "the face of an assassin." When asked if Mendoza was the kind of man to carry out a murder threat, Morillo replied: "he was, certainly, he would be apt to get you before you got him."

Based upon the testimony of Mendoza's character and probable intentions, the jury accepted the shooting as a pre-emptive act of self-defense. Newspaper reporter Rufus K. Porter recounted the trials outcome in correspondence to the *San Francisco Bulletin:*

> The General [Volney E. Howard] made a very eloquent appeal to the jury, and reviewed the testimony very ably. The discharge of Col. Couts was received with much applause and the verdict of "not guilty" pronounced righteous.

The mining camp of Hedges in 1902

The Gold of Hedges

"The gold mines of eastern San Diego county are destined to astonish the world," reported mining expert D. M. Dubraveich in the fall of 1894 as he toured the gold rush town of Hedges, sixteen miles northwest of Yuma. "The people of San Diego," he continued, "do not imagine what a treasure they have in their own county."

The gold mines of Hedges, situated in the desert foothills of the Cargo Muchacho Mountains, never "astonished the world," yet for a time, in the 1890s, the town boomed as the most important gold mining camp in California.

The site of Hedges was discovered in 1884 by Peter Walters, a trackwalker for the Southern Pacific railroad. Little came of the claim, called Gold Rock in the beginning, until several Los Angeles investors bought out Walters for $75,000 and formed the Golden Cross Mining and Milling Company. The firm built a stamp mill to crush ore and a pipeline to draw water from the Colorado River.

Re-christened Hedges in 1893, in honor of the company vice-president, W. V.

The store and offices of the Golden Cross Mining and Milling Company, May 1896

Hedges, the camp quickly grew into a town of over four hundred people. Soon the town boasted of its own post office, public reading room, hospital, hotel, public school house, electric lighting, and "the smallest church (Catholic) in the United States." (While mass was well attended, the saloons and brothels of Hedges did a roaring business.)

The growing community had its share of problems. The Golden Cross Mining and Milling Company ran the town with an iron fist. Prices of goods were high but wages stayed low, averaging three dollars a day. The boarding houses were shabby—one hotel was popularly known as "the hogpen." Working conditions were dangerous—cave-ins, fires, falls, and other assorted accidents claimed several lives. Complaining of mistreatment, one disgruntled miner suggested the company be renamed "the White Man's Slavery Company of California."

If life was hazardous in the mines, it wasn't much safer in the town saloons! In December 1895, two drunken miners were gunned down in Wilson's Saloon, the first of many town homicides. The next year Wilson's was the scene of a fight over a prostitute. One combatant was shot to death.

The presence of a local constable didn't help matters much. In two separate incidents, sheriffs shot and killed men in "self-defense." The coroner labeled the acts "justifiable homicide," the miners called it murder. All told, nearly a dozen men were shot to death in Hedges in five years.

The Golden Cross mines never met their owner's high, original expectations. In a time when gold brought twenty dollars an ounce, Hedges' low-grade ore yielded

Working the tailings at Hedges

only two to five dollars a ton. To boost profits the Golden Cross Company expanded its milling capacity to crush more ore but the action only compounded growing debt problems.

Amid charges of mismanagement, the mines went into court receivership in January 1896. The next year, a Utah syndicate, the Free Gold Mining Company, purchased the properties for one million dollars. The new owners fared marginally better. Thousands of tons of tailings were processed with cyanide to extract more gold. Eventually, however, insolvency loomed and court-appointed receivers took over. By 1905 all mining had ceased and Hedges became a ghost town.

In the years since, there have been no less than five attempts to profit from the old Gold Rock diggings. One firm, the United Mines Company, re-named the site Tumco in 1910 after the company name. As Tumco, the site has been designated a historical landmark by the State Historical Resources Commission. Today, almost nothing remains of San Diego County's toughest mining camp— save a boothill cemetery, collapsing mine shafts, and crumbling adobe walls.

The Whalemen of San Diego Bay

In the early 1850s, a colorful industry emerged in the coastal waters of California. Each winter, from December through February, the southward migration of California gray whales was met by hunters—whalemen who rowed out in longboats to kill the mammals for their oil-rich blubber. Whale oil was a prized commodity in the mid-nineteenth century, valuable for lamp oil and industrial lubricants. To obtain this product, whaling stations sprang up along the coastline from Crescent City to Ensenada. Ballast Point in San Diego Bay was the site of one of the first stations. In San Diego, shore whaling soon became an important industry that would last for three decades.

California shore whaling was the brainchild of one J.P. Davenport, a former New England whaling captain. In 1851 Davenport started a whaling operation at Monterey, which he chartered three years later as the Monterey Whaling Company. From rude tryworks and shanties along shore, the captain and crew sailed and rowed out in thirty-foot whaleboats to capture grays, humpbacks, and killer whales. The whales were dispatched with harpoon guns and bomb lances, then towed ashore to be flensed and rendered. It was a lucrative business from the start, and soon Davenport had competitors in other coastal ports.

San Diego's first whalemen were two brothers of Portuguese descent, Alpheus and Prince Packard. The Packards started their operation on the shores of La Playa at Ballast Point in the winter of 1856-57. A short time later, Captain Miles A. Johnson and his cousins, Henry and James A. Johnson, began another station nearby. The two companies would work side by side until the 1870s. Occasionally they were joined by ocean-going whaleships in the hunt for gray whales. Captain W.W. Clark of the whaler *Ocean* anchored in San Diego for the 1860-61 season and used his ship as a whaling station. Outside the harbor, other whaleships stood off the coast from San Diego to Vizcaino Bay to capture the grays.

The techniques of shore whaling varied little from station to station. Most followed the Davenport model. In San Diego, the whalemen kept their six-man boats off shore throughout the day, waiting for the migration stream to appear in the kelp line off Point Loma. When a gray was sighted, the crews bent to the oars in pursuit then fired their harpoons from bow-mounted swivel guns. After

Flensing a gray whale in San Diego Bay

"getting fast" with a successful strike, the whalemen hauled in the harpoon lines and drew close enough to fire bomb lances from shoulder guns. The bombs were designed to explode within the whale's body and kill instantly.

In practice, the killing of fifty-foot, forty-ton "devil-fish" rarely followed design. All whalemen considered the gray a most difficult and dangerous whale to capture. It took great skill to strike with the harpoon guns and some luck to kill with the hand-held "bum guns." The shoulder guns kicked violently and were known to "fire aft with as much emphasis as forward," frequently hurting the hunter as much as the whale. Bombs often failed, requiring several shots to finish the kill. As a final irony, at least one fifth of all whales killed sank before they could be towed ashore.

Once a gray was successfully taken, there remained the back-breaking task of towing the whale to the station—often from a distance of several miles. The whalemen had to beach the carcasses at high tide, then strip the blubber in large sections. In wooden troughs the blubber was sliced into smaller pieces, then boiled out in 150 gallon iron trypots. Trying out took a dozen men twelve hours for a single whale. When this malodorous process was complete, an average of thirty-five barrels (31.5 gallons per barrel) of "coast oil" was casked for shipment. The oil was usually marketed in San Francisco where it sold for about ten dollars per barrel.

Despite the "villainous stench" created by the trying out process, whale watching became a popular diversion for San Diegans. A favorite January excursion in the 1860s was a picnic at La Playa to view the whalemen at work. But beyond their entertainment value, shore whalemen provided a commercially important product to San Diego— one of the city's few articles of export.

A beached gray whale, 1883

The prosperity of shore whaling varied greatly from year to year. In the 1859-60 season, the Johnsons' station produced 800 barrels of oil worth about $8,000. Yet, only three years later, the county assessor would value their assets at only $1,760. The Packards did not fare much better; in 1865 they were sued in district court by landowner Louis Rose for failing to pay a $700 grocery bill. Often, the industry provided only marginal subsistence to the whalemen.

The two companies' best year came in 1871-72 when they landed over forty whales worth 1,600 barrels of oil. But catches fell markedly in succeeding years— 620 barrels in 1873-74, and only 400 in 1874-75. To boost profits, the whalemen began saving the baleen, or whalebone, from their catches—usually discarded for its poor quality.

The beginning of the end came in 1873 when the whalers were forced to vacate Ballast Point to make room for "government improvements." Captain Johnson resumed operations at North Island on what became known as Whaler's Bight. The Packards, choosing to leave San Diego, moved their base to Santo Tomas below Ensenada. In the next decade, the number of California shore stations dwindled to five—the result of a declining market for whale oil and, more importantly, a rapidly diminishing number of gray whales. In 1885-86, the last reported year of local whaling, the Johnsons landed eight gray whales. The next year, the unique enterprise of San Diego shore whaling was abandoned.

Frank Buck in San Diego

The legendary adventures of Frank "bring 'em back alive" Buck captivated millions of people throughout the world in the 1930s and 40s. Celebrated to this day for his exploits as a wild animal hunter and trader, Buck is less well known for his brief tenure as director of the San Diego Zoo.

Frank J. Buck went to work for the zoo on June 13, 1923. Signed by the Zoological Society to a three-year contract, the forty-one year old Buck came to San Diego backed by the strong recommendation of Dr. William T. Hornaday, director of the famed Bronx Zoo. Three months later, Frank Buck was unceremoniously fired.

Buck decided to sue the Zoological Society and its president, Dr. Harry M.

Frank J. Buck

Wegeforth, for breach of contract. Claiming that he had given up his lucrative animal collecting business to work in San Diego, as well as damage to his reputation, Buck sought damages of $22,500.

In a court deposition filed in January, 1924, Buck recited a litany of grievances, most of them focused upon the actions of Dr. Wegeforth. The zoo president, Buck claimed, had interfered with "practically everything" and had conspired with the Board to "belittle and disparage" his efforts as director. He also alleged that Wegeforth had been responsible for the deaths of 150 snakes that had been force-fed with a sausage stuffer. Buck stated that he had been fired after he built a new bird cage without personal authorization from Wegeforth.

Quite a different story emerged from the testimony of Dr. Wegeforth, board member Thomas N. Faulconer, and several others. All witnesses flatly denied Buck's allegation that snakes had been killed by force-feeding. According to these witnesses Buck's problems stemmed from his unwillingness to consult with the board on everyday policy. Frequently, he deliberately defied board directives. "The whole character of the man," Wegeforth testified, reflected "insubordination."

There was more involved than a clash of wills. Wegeforth charged that Buck was "incompetent" and "could not be trusted." On one occasion Buck had ordered name plates for the animal cages and pens. The order had to be returned when it was found that half of the names had been misspelled by Buck. Wegeforth also cited examples of Buck's failure to recognize disease or properly care for sick animals.

The final straw was an incident involving the zoo's two Indian elephants—Joy and Happy. Buck believed that the hides of the elephants, which appeared dry and cracked, would benefit

Force-feeding a python with a sausage stuffer
Courtesy San Diego Zoological Society

from "oiling," a practice that Dr. Wegeforth knew could cause pneumonia or Bright's disease. Despite the president's orders, Buck oiled the elephants. Wegeforth recalled: "they quickly became very piteous-looking creatures, their trunks grew flaccid and seemed about a foot longer than usual, and their abdomens almost touched the ground. I was afraid they were doomed."

Fortunately, Joy and Happy recovered. Frank Buck, however, was sacked.

On February 20, Superior Court Judge C. N. Andrews ruled against the plaintiff Buck and ordered him to pay court costs of $24. He soon left San Diego and resumed his career as a "zoological collector."

Frank Buck's autobiography, *All in a Lifetime*, does not mention his lawsuit against Wegeforth. Interestingly, "while acting as temporary director of the San Diego Zoo," he does claim credit for inventing a method for force-feeding snakes.

"It's the Water?"

Are you ailing, are you failing,
    Have you ills you cannot tell?
There is healing past revealing
    in the waters of the well.

It is Carlsbad, bonny Carlsbad
    And upon its sparkling brink,
Hygeia sits forever smiling,—-
    And she bids you come and drink.
                    —-*Golden Era, May 1887*

Throughout history the purported medicinal value of mineral water has attracted people to natural springs. In the late 1800s, "health seekers" flocked to southern California, often to drink or bathe in the healthful local waters—such as the mineral springs of Carlsbad, California.

Carlsbad owes much of its early renown to a sea captain, John A. Frazier, who came to the area in 1883 and settled on a government homestead. Frazier drilled two wells by his home and struck water at just over four hundred feet. Frazier soon decided his well water had remarkable curative powers over his chronic rheumatism.

As a small village called Frazier's Station grew around the railroad depot for the California Southern Railroad (later Santa Fe), Frazier offered his water to railroad passengers traveling between Los Angeles and San Diego. A huge water barrel near the depot boasted a sign inviting travelers to "alight, drink and be happy."

One traveler who "alighted" at Frazier's Station in 1885 was a German-born merchant from the Midwest named Gerhard Schutte. The great southern California land "boom of the 80s" had brought Schutte, his wife, and nine children, to California in search of a town of "small farms and gracious homes." Frazier's Station seemed to be ideal. For forty dollars an acre, Schutte bought John Frazier's land and became a town builder.

In partnership with several others, Schutte bought up several hundred acres around Frazier's Station. To promote the town-site, the partners decided to

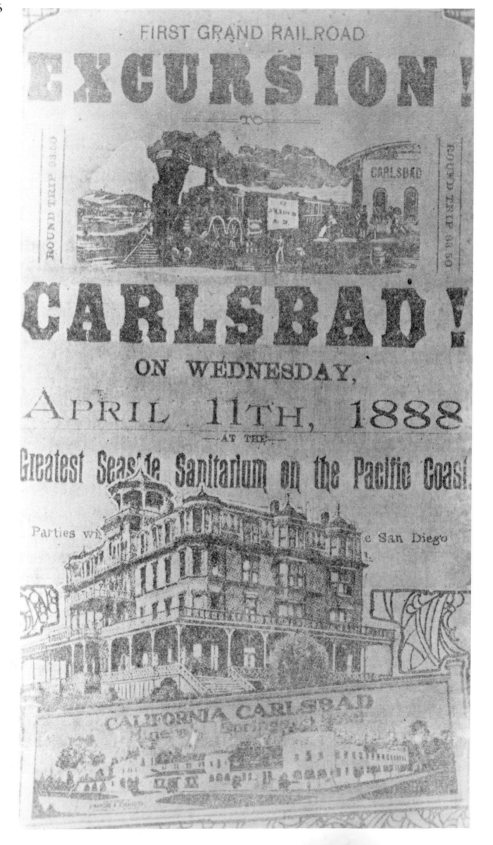

Founders of Carlsbad stand on the railroad platform near the Hotel Carlsbad: (left to right) John Frazier, Mrs. Frazier, Rebecca Frazier, Gerhard Schutte, Samuel Church Smith, and D. D. Wadsworth

advertise the local mineral water as an attraction. To their delight, chemical analysis of the water proved it to be almost identical to the celebrated water of "Well Number Nine" at Europe's world-famous spa at Karlsbad, Bohemia (in modern Czechoslovakia). The partners named their enterprise the Carlsbad Land and Mineral Water Company. Frazier's Station, predictably enough, was re-named Carlsbad.

An intensive publicity campaign followed, based on the curative potency of Carlsbad mineral water. An eight-page brochure circulated nationally, extolling water "from the bosom of Nature." The region's climate was also praised, suggesting that strawberries could be picked from April through Christmas. "Is this not as near Eden as any the world has ever seen?" asked the boosters.

Carlsbad mineral water was even endorsed by the County Physician, Dr. J. P. Le Feure, who commented in his annual report for 1889 that Carlsbad was "one of the most healthy locations in the state." "Numerous testimonials from many invalids," added Le Feure, "show that these waters have produced marked improvement in health in a short time from their use."

San Diego's *Golden Era* magazine predicted Carlsbad was "destined to occupy a foremost place among the great sanitariums of the world....it is safe to say that no other resort in the world combines the peculiar advantages for the health and pleasure seeker to be found there."

John Frazier's water tower supplied mineral water to Hotel Carlsbad.
Courtesy Carlsbad Public Library

For a time, the advertising certainly succeeded. With real estate booming in all of southern California, "no town on the California Southern Railroad [grew] faster than Carlsbad." After only six months of life, the town could claim its own newspaper (*The Sea Lion*), telegraph and post offices, an elaborate Victorian-style train depot, two churches, an elementary school, a small hotel, and two hundred residents. To replace the one inadequate hotel, the Carlsbad Land and Mineral Water Company started construction on a eighty-five room, four-story hotel.

But as the "elegant, commodious" Carlsbad Hotel opened in late 1887, the real estate bubble was bursting. The special excursion trains brought by real estate agents to Carlsbad ended. Land prices slid throughout San Diego County.

The Carlsbad Hotel continued to draw tourists and "health seekers," attracted by the fine beaches, easy railroad transportation, and, of course, the water. But in 1896, the hotel burned, some thought by arson.

The community survived, well-served by its mild climate and magnificent setting. And the popularity of Carlsbad water continued for decades as bottled mineral water was shipped throughout the West.

Today, the site of John Frazier's original well is preserved beneath Alt Karlsbad, a replica of a German Hanseatic house, on Carlsbad Boulevard.

The Real "Ramona"

Sam Temple, ca. 1900

In the fall of 1883, novelist Helen Hunt Jackson, writing from her home in Colorado, penned a letter to a friend in San Diego:

> I'm going to write an Indian novel, the scene laid in So. California. I would rather you did not speak of this, as I shall keep it a secret, until the book is done.

Less than a year later, Jackson's romantic novel, *Ramona*, appeared in print. It has been a perennial best-seller ever since.

Set in the backcountry of northern San Diego County, the novel was inspired by several actual incidents, particularly, the murder of an Indian by a white rancher in March, 1883.

Juan Diego, a Cahuilla Indian, lived with his wife and small child near the Cahuilla Indian Reservation in the San Jacinto Mountains. He was known as a "locoed" Indian—crazy at times though not dangerous.

One evening Juan returned home from his work as a sheepshearer riding a strange horse. When his wife asked about the horse, Juan replied, in confusion, "where is my horse then?" He realized he had left his own mount in the corral and taken a similar horse by mistake. Juan's wife, frightened by the error, said, "you must take that horse right back; they will say you stole it."

Juan never got the chance. Sam Temple, owner of the mistaken horse, rode up to the house and called out to Juan.

> [Temple] poured out a volley of oaths, leveled his gun and shot him dead. After Juan had fallen on the ground Temple rode closer and fired three more shots in the body, one in the forehead, one in the cheek, and one in the wrist...He then took his horse, which was standing tied in front of the house, and rode away.

Temple surrendered himself to the local justice of the peace—a fellow rancher named S. V. Tripp. Before a jury of twelve white men, Temple claimed that Juan Diego had attacked him with a knife. The jurors visited the site of the killing and listened to Temple's story. Eyewitness testimony from Juan's wife and two other Native American witnesses was ignored. Ruling the action "justifiable homicide," justice Tripp ordered Temple released.

One juror summed up the popular feeling by saying, "I don't care whether the Indian had a knife or not…Any man that'd take a horse of mine and ride up that mountain trail, I'd shoot him wherever I found him." The juror did concede that "Temple was to blame for firin' into him after he was dead. That was mean, I'll allow."

Sam Temple (standing) with justice of the peace S.V. Tripp

In Helen Hunt Jackson's novel, Juan Diego served as a prototype for the tragic victim, Alessandro. The rancher Sam Temple was transformed into the evil Jim Ferrar. The wife of Juan Diego became Ramona, heroine of the romance.

Until his death Sam Temple reveled in his notoriety as "the man who killed Alessandro." He also continued to skirmish with the law. Over the years Temple fought off charges in the courts for disturbing the peace, assault with a deadly weapon, and attempted murder.

The "historical" Ramona is most often suggested to be Ramona Lubo, who lived in the San Jacinto region until her death in 1922. Renowned for her basketry, Ramona Lubo's work was exhibited at San Diego's California-Pacific International Exposition in 1935. Ramona Lubo herself was often "displayed" at county fairs where tourists came to gawk at "the original Ramona."

Since 1884, the novel *Ramona* has been reprinted more than 300 times. There have been four different film versions of the story (the best known version starred Don Ameche with Loretta Young) and, in the community of Hemet, an outdoor stage play—the Ramona Pageant—has been produced annually since 1923.

Jackson wrote *Ramona* in the hope that it would "stir people up" and awaken public sympathy toward the plight of San Diego Indians. Instead, her novel fostered the enduring myth of "the Ramona country."

Frontier San Diego: The Letters of Thomas Darnall

Among the many young, ambitious men who came to San Diego at the time of the California gold rush, was one Thomas Rylan Darnall of Clark County, Kentucky. A failure at gold mining in northern California, Darnall came to San Diego in 1853 and opened a store. At the age of twenty-eight he chaired the County Board of Supervisors and also served as deputy sheriff.

The following excerpts are taken from letters Darnall wrote to his family in Kentucky. They provide a valuable glimpse of frontier San Diego of the 1850s. The complete transcripts can be found in the Darnall Collection of the Research Archives.

Thomas Ryland Darnall

Brother James: San Diego, October 18th, 1855

...If we only had some of the society here, that we find in the older states, then we would have the greatest country in the whole world, even without the Rail Road. There is but one american girl in the place unmarried who is grown, and she can neither read or write; scarcely any of the native Californians can read or write. We have the most healthy and salubrious climate in the world; I have been here nearly three years, and have not seen more than six or seven funerals, and most of those deaths were caused by imprudence. We frequently have a baile (ball) to while away the time, the Californian girls are great for dancing; their principal dancing consists in waltz and polkas, in the execution of which they excel any girls I ever saw; they likewise beat all creation in eating, a party of twenty Californian girls will eat more than one hundred american girls. As the women excel in dancing so the men excel in horsemanship, they are by far the most superior horsemen I ever saw, even the boys three or four and five years of age are expert...

San Diego Aug. 5th 1856

Usually, we have the most mild climate in the world, but for the last few days it has been intensely hot, and to alleviate the sultriness, I go bathing, almost every evening, in the ocean, and every Sunday certain for the girls go along, and Oh! what a luscious time! "We does has"; that is a luxury I never enjoyed in the States. We have the nicest beach in the world for bathing with just sufficient breakers to make it interesting and pleasant. It is very dangerous bathing in the bay on account of a kind of fish called, here, stingaree, which lays flat on the bottom, it takes its name from a sharp boney substance, resembling a needle, appended to its tail; and when tread upon or molested will strike with great force, its stroke is immediately followed by great pain, accompanied with swelling of the wounded part; it has never to my knowledge been found only in smooth- water, so to evade its attacks we go to the breakers outside of the bay. You must not imagine, because it is not customary, in your country, for men and women to bathe together, that the women here are more immoral or indecent then there, such is not the case; custom makes laws, and as it is a custom to bathe together here we can see no impropriety in its indulgence.

Father and Mother: September 13th, 1857

...I have entered into a copper mining speculation in Mexico, and have invested every cent that I can call my own and a little more. I feel confident that I have a good show to make a grand raise. I have had quite a serious difficulty with the Mexican authorities during the last month, I was confined in prison for twelve days in a very precarious situation. I send you some papers containing the details—If it had not been for this difficulty we would now have between six thousand and ten thousand dollars worth of ore on the way to the market, but now I do not know when we will be able to ship the ore. I have two joint partners in the mining operation. Aside from the mining speculation my prospects are very flattering. I have a considerable amount invested in San Diego property, which I think shall be very valuable in a short time...

Thomas Darnall's hopes were never realized in San Diego. After his problems with Mexican authorities, he sold his interest in the "Jesus Maria" mine for $400. He returned east to his family in 1859 and settled finally in Platte, Missouri. Darnall died in Platte in 1906.

The Renegade Republican

Few San Diego elections have been more colorful than the mayoral campaign of 1905. A bitter, partisan affair, it pitted an establishment Republican, Danville F. Jones, against an Independent, Captain John L. Sehon. It was also a fight between two rival newspapers: John D. Spreckels' *San Diego Union* and E. W. Scripps' *San Diego Sun.*

Mayor John L. Sehon

The political climate in America was changing in 1905. A year earlier Theodore Roosevelt had been re-elected President on a wave of reform spirit. Civic-minded progressives throughout the country attacked government corruption and promoted social and economic reform. In San Diego, reformers forced changes in the City Charter which reduced the number of councilmen from twenty-seven to nine and provided for the initiative, recall, and referendum—measures the *Union* called "socialistic."

The *Union* was particularly alarmed when Sehon, a retired Army officer and councilman, decided to run for a two- year term as mayor. Nominated by the Independents and supported by Democrats and progressive Republicans, Sehon promised an end to "bossism" in San Diego. The *Union* indignantly labeled Sehon a "renegade Republican."

However, Sehon was strongly supported by the *Sun.* The newspaper's endorsement stemmed at least partly from Sehon's desire to push water development in the El Cajon Valley on lands that just happened to be owned by E. W. Scripps. The *Union* quite naturally opposed the El Cajon development since Spreckels had his own plans for selling water to the city.

On election day, April 4, Sehon upset Jones by a margin of 2018 votes to 1376. A Socialist candidate, W. J. Kirkwood, gathered 438 votes.

San Diego City Hall, 5th & G.

The reformers had won the election but the Republican machine refused to concede. A suit was filed in Superior Court that challenged the right of a retired military officer to take both a government pension and a mayor's $1,200 per year salary. Judge E. S. Torrance ordered Sehon subpoenaed but when Deputy Sheriff Henry Cook attempted to serve the papers, the mayor-elect could not be found.

Captain Sehon re-appeared at 2:00 in the morning on May 1, the day he was scheduled to replace Frank P. Frary as mayor. Accompanied by several friends, the ex-infantry officer forced open the doors of City Hall at 5th and G Streets, smashed the glass door leading to the mayor's chambers, and claimed possession of his new office.

Two days later, Judge Torrance declared Sehon ineligible for public office and his election null and void. The new mayor ignored the verdict and calmly conducted city business while the case was appealed. On October 23, the State District Court of Appeal reversed Torrance's ruling.

John Sehon served out an eventful term, marked by the *Bennington* disaster and the San Francisco earthquake, unhindered by the chastened Republican machine.

Forster's Rancho Santa Margarita

The Great Drought

The climate was bone dry…There was no moisture and our cattle died off in very great numbers…Before the year 1864 had passed away, there was perfect devastation. Such a thing was never before known in California. —Juan Forster, Rancho Santa Margarita.

Droughts are common in California, always have been. Long before scientists suggested a "greenhouse effect" or the vagaries of "El Nino," pioneers coped with erratic and disastrous wet/dry cycles. The drought of 1862-65 was a catastrophe for the state of California—a bitter dry period, preceded by unusually heavy rains and accompanied by an untimely epidemic of smallpox.

The decade of the 1860s began with little hint of the natural catastrophes ahead. For several years in succession gentle fall and winter rains had fallen with consistency, supporting vast grasslands that fed immense herds of cattle. But in the winter of 1861-62 rains of biblical proportions came to California.

The rain fell for almost a month, inundating river valleys, farmlands, and towns. The persistency of the rain led the editor of the Los Angeles *Star* to comment: "On Tuesday last the sun made its appearance. The phenomenon lasted several minutes and was witnessed by a great number of persons."

Juan Forster

In San Diego the flooding washed away soil and timberlands, destroyed vineyards, melted adobe houses, and drowned livestock. At San Luis Rey the raging floods "cut an arroyo fifty feet across." An estimated 200,000 head of cattle were lost in California.

But in the spring the rain-soaked grazing lands flourished. In the abundant pasturage, herds of cattle recovered quickly.

Then came three years of intense drought. In the fall and winter of 1862-63 only 3.87 inches of rain fell in San Diego County. As the grasslands dried up the long-horned steers grew emaciated and weak. The overstocked ranchers tried to minimize their losses by thinning their herds. The markets became flooded with cowhides and prices fell.

From Santa Margarita (modern day Camp Pendleton), rancher Juan Forster would write in January 1863: "We poor Rancheros have had a damned bad string of luck these last two years and if it is going to continue I don't know what will become of us." To cut losses Forster drove his herds into the mountains, saving perhaps half his cattle.

At Rancho Guajome near San Luis Rey, rancher Cave Couts complained, "What are the cattle raisers going to do? No grass, nearly as dry as in the month of August...Not only want of pasture, but Small-pox allows no general *recogidas* this spring."

The outbreak of smallpox in California added human misery to the growing economic toll. Appearing in the fall of 1862, the plague quickly spread throughout southern California. Effective quarantines proved impossible and vaccine could only be obtained from San Francisco.

Cave Couts reported: "Small pox is quite prevalent—six to eight per day are being buried in S. Juan Capistrano—Indians generally...I vaccinated the whole rancheria at San Luis some six weeks since, & hope they may escape, thus saving our community of the terrible disease."

By late spring the smallpox epidemic had run its course, but the drought continued. A little more than five inches of rain fell in 1863-64. More and more ranchers drove their cattle into the mountains in the search for grass and water. Other cattlemen moved their herds to Baja California. From San Luis Rey, Couts would moan: "I am badly in want of money...taxes on hand, no goods in my shop & no money."

GUAJOME, HOME OF THE LATE COL. CAVE. J. COUTS 4 MILES EAST OF THE MISSION SAN LUIS REY, SAN DIEGO CO. CALA

As the drought lingered the bad luck of ranchers continued. A violent storm that broke in May killed famished cattle grazing in the mountains. Forster lost three hundred head in one night at Santa Ysabel. When summer came, strong dry winds were reported and grasshoppers appeared which soon stripped the remaining forage.

The drought finally began to ease in November 1864. Two and a half inches of rain fell, followed by over five inches in the next two months. Not until the twelve-inch season of 1864-65 did the cattlemen feel secure.

The Great Drought virtually ruined the once great cattle industry of California. Statewide the herds declined by about 46 percent in the 1860s. The numbers are unknown for San Diego County but in Los Angeles the loss was over 70 percent.

The long-term impact did show a few benefits. Ranchers learned to plant feed crops in order to lessen their reliance upon natural forage. The raising of sheep (a far more "drought- tolerant" animal than a cow!) became popular. In northern San Diego County a more diversified agricultural economy slowly developed.

Inquisition by Coroner's Jury.

State of California, } ss.
County of San Diego,

In the matter of the Inquisition upon
the body of

David Blair
Deceased.

Before *L. L. Wilcox Acting* Coroner.

We, the undersigned, the jurors summoned to appear before *L. L. Wilcox Acting* the Coroner of the County of San Diego, at *Agua Caliente Hot Spring* on the *29th* day of *July* A. D. 188*7*, to inquire into the cause of the death of *one David Blair* having been duly sworn according to law, and having made such inquisition, after inspecting the body, and hearing the testimony adduced, upon our oaths, each and all do say that we find the deceased was named *David Blair* was a native of *unknown* aged about *55* years; that he came to his death on the *About 30th* day of *June* A. D. 188*7*, in this County, by *a blow on his left Jaw by some heavy Weapon which broke the Jaw Bone and Chick Bone and two Knife wounds on the left side of the Neck which was the cause of Death and we the Jury Charge Oliver Rilley (Colored) with the Crime of willfull Murder of deceased David Blair*

All of which we duly certify by this inquisition, in writing, by us signed, this *29th* day of *July* A. D. 188*7*.

Raphaël Roy

B. J. Davis

A. Parker

James H Page Foreman

I hereby Certify that this Inquiry was held and the verdict has my approval L. L. Wilcox Justice of the Peace Acting Coroner

Turner Helm x

H H Davis

L. W. Littlefield

Henry D. Wilkes

N. M. Bradfield

George Davis

Mike Cronin

A. L. Hooker

The verdict of a coroner's jury, 29 July 1887

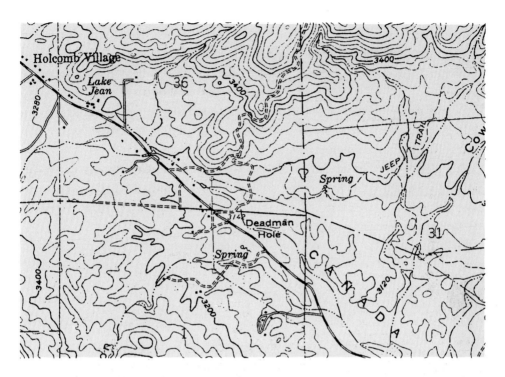

"Deadman's Hole"

In Erwin Gudde's classic *California Place Names*, the author notes more than a score of California locales bearing the macabre name of "Deadman." Throughout California, many canyons, creeks, islands, flats, and gulches, have been dubbed "Deadman"—a convenient term for places where a corpse was found.

San Diego's "Deadman's Hole," is located in the northeast county along Highway 79, midway between Warner Springs and Oak Grove. Modern topographic maps from the U.S. Geological Survey show the site about one mile southeast of Sunshine Summit.

For much of the late 1800s, the historic Butterfield Stage passed through this region. A spring of water at the site of the Hole made it a popular rest stop.

A Butterfield stagecoach paused here in 1858. Reportedly, as the stage driver knelt down by the spring for a drink of cool water he was horrified by the staring face of a man, bobbing lifeless in the water. From that day forward, the area would bear the name of Deadman's Hole.

A mysterious murder occurred here in June 1887. One Oliver Reilly discovered a miner's camp, neatly laid out but apparently abandoned. Two mules, nearly dead from thirst, stood tied to a nearby tree. A journal of Mr. D. Blair was found at the camp.

Days later, the corpse of David Blair was found at the spring of Deadman's Hole. A hastily convened coroner's jury blamed the killing on Oliver Reilly. The hapless Reilly was eventually released for lack of evidence.

Only months later Deadman's Hole was the scene of another strange death. An Indian girl named Belita was found strangled. Two months later, her stepfather, Luis Melendrez—known as "Chihuahua"—was arrested near Julian. The case was apparently never prosecuted.

Yet a third murder occurred almost simultaneously. The body of a woman named Franciscia Ranteria, aged 45, was discovered close to the same spot where David Blair had been found. The coroner's jury found two bullet wounds in her back, "inflicted by some person or persons unknown."

Certainly the strangest story of Deadman's Hole was reported in the *San Diego Union* in 1888. Two hunters from Julian, Edward Dean and Charles Cox spotted "an immense unwieldy animal, that from a rear view resembled a bear." It might have been a bear but the creature walked upright. The men followed the animal into an area known today as Dark Canyon. To stop the creature they fired shots in the air. "The beast stopped and turned to face its pursuers...They saw before them a human countenance..."

The hunters killed the beast and then discovered its lair. "Cox struck a match and by its blaze all the mysteries in Deadman's Hole were revealed." The cave was filled with skeletal remains, including five human skulls. Thus, declared the *Union*, the mysterious deaths at Deadman's Hole were solved. The strange beast had been the culprit. The creature was loaded into a wagon and hauled to San Diego for public exhibition.

On April 2, the day after the story was first reported, the newspaper ran another short article that reported that many people had gone to the San Diego police station to view the remains. They had all been told to come back the following year for the next "April Fool's" day.

Vigilante Justice
In San Diego

California had little trouble convicting and executing its murderers in the late 1800s—a violent period in San Diego history, particularly in rural and isolated north county areas. After brief trials, most condemned slayers from San Diego were hanged on the grounds of the county courthouse. Appeals and stays of execution were rare. (After 1893, the condemned from all counties were executed at San Quentin. The first man executed at the state prison was a San Diegan—Jose Gabriel, hanged for murdering a farm family from Otay.)

Occasionally, public anger over a heinous crime provoked "popular justice" or "vigilantism." Lynching by vigilantes proved to be a popular alternative in the mid-nineteenth century to the unpredictable verdicts from court trials.

The first known incidence of vigilantism in San Diego occurred in 1853 following the murder of an indigent tailor named John Warren. Found bludgeoned by the jawbone of an ox, the coroner's jury ruled the death occurred from "wounds inflicted by some person or persons unknown." Six months later, townspeople led by E. W. Morse and Robert Israel, rounded up three Native Americans suspected of the crime. Without a trial, two of the suspects were hanged in Old Town. The third Indian escaped.

In December 1875, a bloody gunbattle in Campo led to San Diego County's best known case of vigilantism. Two Sonorans captured in the attempted robbery of Gaskill's Store—Jose Elvira and Raphael Garcia—were taken from their jail cell at night and hanged on a tree from a single piece of rope. The jailer, Jerry Gaskill, claimed to the coroner's jury that while guarding the prisoners a "gang of men came into the room...tied my hands and took the prisenor out of the room. That is all I no of the prisenors now deceased."

The year 1878 was a busy one for "popular" justice. In the gold rush town of Julian, an Indian named Juan La Cruz was jailed for attacking a woman and her child while "crazed with drink." Although the woman and child were unhurt, nightfall brought an excited crowd to the town jail where they demanded the prisoner. When the guard refused, the mob threw a sack over his head and seized the prisoner.

The next morning the body of Juan La Cruz was discovered hanging in the woods nearby. As a crowd gathered one witness spoke up: "You've done a good job, you reformers. Now why don't you hang the man who sold the whiskey to the Indian?"

In July, a rancher named William Palmerston was attacked and killed by an intruder in his home in the San Jacinto Valley. The slayer, identified as Refugio Baca, was captured the next day by a sheriff's posse. The alleged murderer sat in a Temecula jail cell and waited for a justice court hearing scheduled for the following morning.

The local citizenry planned a different future for Baca. That night a crowd of "20 or 30 masked men," carrying shotguns, rifles, and pistols, removed Baca from his guards, fastened a rope around his neck and hanged him from the limb of a cottonwood tree. The following day a hurriedly summoned coroner's jury rendered their verdict: "Refugio Baca came to his Death by hanging by the neck to a rope the same being executed by unknown Parties, the same Generaly known as a Mob."

Later that year an Indian "desperado" known as Jose Laguna, alias "Ramon," was arrested near Warner's Ranch and brought to San Diego. Charged with attempted murder in another county, a nervous Ramon asked his courthouse jailer if there "were vigilantes here like there was in Los Angeles."

The following day the Indian was found dangling from the

The San Diego Union.

Evening Edition.

SAN DIEGO, MONDAY EVENING, DECEMBER 6th, 1875.

THE CAMPO RAID.

SURRENDER OF ONE OF THE WOUNDED BANDITS.

The Supposed Customer Proves to be One of the Outlaws.

THE CORONER'S INQUEST

Capture of the Entire Gang Probable.

"A GOOD DAY'S WORK"

Special Dispatch to The San Diego Union.

CAMPO, December 5.—About four o'clock this morning one of the Mexicans who was shot by Mr. L. H. Gaskill crawled up to the house and begged to be taken in. He had been out in the brush hiding; but the cold morning made him seek shelter. He was thought to be in a dying condition, and the people, pitying him, took him in and made him a bed near a warm fire. Five buckshot wounds were found on the right side,—three in the proximity of the lung, and two lower down in the abdomen. There are also two wounds in his right arm. His case is hopeless, as Dr Millard thinks he cannot live till midnight.

The other Mexican, whom we all thought innocent, was proved to be one of the gang, and the one who ran to head off Mr. S. E. Gaskill, but whom Mr. Gaskill shot. His condition this evening is much better. As he is able to sit up, Sheriff Hunsaker has put him in irons, locking a large twenty-foot iron chain to one of his ankles. He will be taken to San Diego by to-morrow's stage. He has told so many different stories, and contradicted himself so much, it is hard to tell what his name is, or what his relations were with the band. He told Silas Gaskill that if he would clear him he would work for him twelve years without pay.

turned this afternoon, and reported that they had not heard or seen anything of them. It is thought they struck over through Starvation Valley, and went to Las Juntas. Mr. Gonzales, the Alcalde who lives just over the line, will start out with a party to-night in search of them. He says he is confident capture or track them before morning.

A GOOD DAY'S WORK.

Of the three bandits who got away, we are positive that two are severely wounded, one being shot through the neck with a pistol ball, and the other shot in the breast and neck with buckshot. Of the other three, one was shot dead, and two are at this place wounded. We can therefore claim a good day's work.

CORONER'S INQUEST.

Justice Cline served in the capacity of Coroner to-day at the inquest held over the remains of the dead man. Twelve jurymen were sworn, who viewed the body. Several witnesses were then called who testified concerning the outrage and the mannner of the death. The following verdict was rendered: "We the jury do find that deceased came to his death from the effects of nine buckshot wounds in the right breast at the hands of Mr. Silas E. Gaskill, and we further find that the act was justifiable as it was done in self-defense." A rude box was constructed in which the remains were placed, and they were buried.

MR. GASKILL'S CONDITION.

Dr. Millard arrived about 11:30 last night. He proceeded immediately to the house of Mr. L. H. Gaskill, and commenced the treatment of his case. He reports Mr. Gaskill's injury as being of a very serious character, but has strong hopes of his recovery. The wound does not seem to pain him any, and he rests very easy.

SEARCH FOR THE OTHER BANDITS.

The party of ten, who went out in search of the remainder of the band, re-

LATER.

JUDGE LYNCH AT CAMPO.

The Guard Overpowered and the Prisoners Hung.

CAMPO, December 6.—Last night, at eleven o'clock, a party of unknown men overpowered and tied the Sheriff's guard, seized the two Mexican prisoners and hung them.

Coroner's jury verdict in the lynching of Refugio Baca

rafters of his cell with his feet bound and his hands tied behind him. A coroner's jury rendered a remarkable verdict: "he came to his death by hanging himself."

Nearly all known cases of vigilante action in San Diego County in the nineteenth century involved either Hispanics or Native Americans as victims. And in each incident the coroner's jury failed to indict perpetrators.

Lynch law seldom meant justice in frontier San Diego. But the law was certainly swift!

Fever & Ague

Peruvian Bark 2 oz Wild Cherry tree Bark
one oz Cinamon Bark one drachm
Capsicum one Tea spoon full Sulphur
one oz Port wine 2 qts let it stand 2
days Bee sure & Get Genuine Ingrediences
dose one wine Glass full Every 2 or 3 Hours after
the Fever is off then 2 or three times a day till it
is all used up & it is a certain Cure keep the Bowels
Well Clensed & open

Starch Polish

one Part of White wax & two Parts of
Sperma ceti & mold in small cakes Directions
Put into a Pint of Starch a Piece the size of a
Pea & it will Give a Beautifull Polish & keep the Iron from
Sticking

Tooth Paste

Suds of Castile Soap & Spts of Camphor
of Each Equal quantities thicken with
Equal Parts of Pulverized Chalk & Charcoal
to a thick Paste Aply with the Finger or Brush

Fly Poison Paper

Take 2 oz of dry Starch in Powder & add one oz
of Arsenic & mix Completly together then
make them into a thin Sutution of With Sweetened
Watter then dip Comon Brown Paper in to
it & Saturate Completely & then Hang up to dry.
then Directions lay a Piece onto a Plate & add a little Watter

Salve Pure Vegatable

Lard one lb Rosin ½ lb Elder Bark
Ten oz Boil them over a Slow fire 10 minutes or
half Hour then Strain & Put in Boxes

Frontier Medicine

Luman H. Gaskill

Pioneer ledger books often record more than business activities. The ledger of Campo storekeeper Luman H. Gaskill, kept in the late 1880s, is a remarkable compendium of home remedies and household notes, as well as store receipts and accounts.

Storekeeper, banker, marshall, justice of the peace, dentist, and doctor, Luman Gaskill was a versatile frontiersmen who recorded everything from "how to detect Spurious Greenbacks" to how to "Break a Dog from Sucking Eggs."

Gaskill's ledger advises that to tenderize beef one should parboil the meat in vinegar; to rid the house of cockroaches pulverized borax will do the trick; to preserve eggs simply grease the eggs with "vegatable greese and lay a way." There is even a novel method of measuring a tree's height:

> walk from the tree looking at it from time to time Between your knees with your Back towards the tree & as soon as you are able to see the top of the tree in this way your distance from the root is Equal to the higth.

The highlight of the Gaskill ledger book is the many home medical remedies for every possible ailment likely to afflict a San Diego pioneer. With the flu and cold season upon us, we herein include a sampler of folk medicine from "Dr. Gaskill:"

TO CURE TOOTHAKE
take a ½ Sheet of Brown Paper & twist it
up like a lamp liter & place the small
End in the Cavity in the tooth then Set the other
End a fire & hold it in as long as Posibal.

FLUX OF DIAREA
take Wheat flour & Parch it same as
you would Coffee & mix it with Scalded
milk is an Excellant thing

Opposite page: A page from the ledger of Luman Gaskill

The Gaskill Brothers store in Campo

CHOUGH RECIEPT
take Strong vinegar 1 qt
Put in alarge mouth Bottle and
Put in 3 hole Eggs not Breaking them
and When the vinegar Eats them up
then ad 1 pt Honey take a swallow
When Ever you feel a tickling in your throat

CURE FOR CANKER SORE MOUTH
take an old Boot or Shoe Sole and
Burn it and take the ashes and
mix a little Honey With them Enough
to make a Salve then Oint your mouth
3 or 4 times a day *Sure Cure*

ANOTHER [CANKER SORE]
take 10 drops of Creasoot in
a glass of Watter and wash with
throat 3 times a day

CURE FOR FRESH WOUNDS
take some live coals on a shovel
and Sprinkle Some Brown
Sugar and let the Smoke go
on the Sore Hold the Wound over
the Smoke until it is Well Smoked
& the Pain will leave very soon

PILES
take Tobacco and Burn it
then Take the ashes and Mix with Lard
and oint the affected part

SOAR THROAT
Take 30 drops or teaspoons
full of Creasoot put it in
1 pint of Watter wash the throat
3 or 4 times a day it ~~wont hurt to~~
~~swallow some~~

TO CURE EARACHE
take a comon sized onion
and roast it take the out side
until the center will go in the Ear
Slip it in the Ear as hot as posibal

RATTLESNAKE BITE
Rub the wound full of Gunpowder
and then Pour on a good Charge on the top of
all and then Put fire to it and Burn it
that will Cure it on all dum brutes

TO CURE HABITUAL DRUNKENESS
When Whiskey gits the Best of aman and he
cant quit Drinking this will Distroy all Desire
for liquor
Sulphate of Iron 5 Grains
Magnesia 10 Grains
Peppermint Watter 11 Drachms
Spirits of Nutmeg 1 Drachm
to Be taken 2 a day

TOBACO ANTIDOTE
take Genitan root a Small Piece
& Chew & Swallow the juice
takes away all the apetite for Tobacco

CURE FOR FEVOR AND AGUE
take a nutmeg grated fine
and a Piece of alum the size of a nutmeg
and Hlaf a Pint of vinegar an
Simmer until alum is desolved
then drink when the Chill Comes

The Indian reservation at Pala

The Mysterious Death of Manuel Olegario

"The danger is imminent," proclaimed an excited reporter for the *San Diego Union*, "a conflict may occur at any moment between the desperate Indians under the control of Olegario."

In October 1875, an Indian war seemed ready to erupt in northern San Diego county. "A thousand warriors" led by the Luiseño chieftain Olegario appeared to threaten the settlers of the San Luis Rey Valley. Only two years after the bloody Modoc War in northern California, it seemed that San Diegans might also see violence.

For years San Diego Indians had fought federal proposals to force them onto reservations established at San Pasqual and Pala. The elected leader of the Luiseños, Manuel Olegario, feared the loss of traditional lands and advised his people to remain on their small ancestral *rancherias*.

Olegario's strong stand created resentment among the white settlers of the San Luis Rey Valley who were eager to appropriate valuable tracts of Indian land. Olegario was also disliked for his ouster of a white-appointed Indian, Manuel Cota. The elderly Cota was despised by most Indians for his weak leadership and unquestioning deference to white authority.

If the whites feared Olegario, they also respected his abilities. Indian agent John G. Ames wrote in an 1874 report to Congress: "He is intelligent, above average, peacefully disposed toward whites, capable of controlling his Indians . . .and is at the same time an enthusiastic defender of his people and disposed to take advanced grounds on questions of their rights."

Tensions seemed to diminish in November, when newspapers reported that Olegario was traveling to Washington, D.C. to visit President Grant. The President promised the chief relief and protection for his people. On December 27, by executive order, over 52,000 acres of land were granted to the Indians of San Diego County.

But confrontation continued. In the next two years Olegario fought constantly to preserve Indian land against white encroachment. By the summer of 1877, the newspapers again proclaimed an "impending Indian outbreak." Tension rose when Olegario and fifty followers forcefully removed white ranchers from Indian land near Pala. Settlers demanded the arrest of Olegario and the eviction of Indians from their small tracts of land.

In July 1877, as newspapers warned of "a collision likely to happen at any moment . . ." Olegario was found dead. The chief had apparently expired in his sleep. The Luiseños immediately claimed their leader had been poisoned. A chorus of Indian protests demanded that authorities agree to an autopsy.

The local justice of the peace, William Couts, and County Coroner Thomas C. Stockton, agreed to exhume the body and perform an examination. However, contrary to state law, they failed to summon a coroner's jury. The two men found no trace of poison and reported that death had been caused by a ruptured blood vessel.

The epilogue to the death of Olegario was as strange as his demise. A petition from forty-six of San Diego's more prominent citizens was sent to the County Board of Supervisors. The petitioners were irate that county funds had been expended on the inquest.

In a document that reveals the racial attitudes of San Diegans in the 1870s, the petitioners offered several reasons for their formal protest:

1st. The Indian died in a perfectly natural way for an Indian.

2nd. He was not a citizen or Taxpayer of this state or county.

3rd. The United States has exclusive control of Indians, they are not subject to our laws, but are governed by Tribal laws of their own...

The petition concluded by adding that there were two thousand of "this worthless population" in San Diego County and it was not the people's business to "dig up Indians" or inquire into what "particular vice killed them."

The County Supervisors dismissed the petition without comment. And to this day, Luiseño Indians question the death of Olegario.

Petition to the San Diego County Board of Supervisors, 1877

The Spanish Flu

In the fall of 1918 a popular verse could be heard in the City of San Diego:

> I had a little bird,
> Its name was Enza.
> I opened the window,
> And in-flu-enza.

In the months following the end of World War I, the "Spanish Influenza" swept the world, infecting a billion people and killing 20 million. In San Diego the scourge reached epidemic proportions in November and December of 1918. There were 4,392 cases that year out of a population of about 70,000; 324 people died.

The disease baffled doctors but city health officers recommended the standard precautions—quarantine and gauze masks. On December 5, 1918, the City Council imposed a general quarantine that closed schools, theaters, and churches, and banned all public gatherings. Days later the councilmen passed another ordinance "requiring the universal use of gauze masks within the City of San Diego." Soon San Diegans had another rhyme:

> Obey the laws
> And wear the gauze.
> Protect your jaws
> From septic paws.

The councilmen required masks of 4-ply surgical gauze fastened over the mouth and nose by strings tied behind the head. In a pinch, 6-ply cheesecloth was acceptable. The gauze was thought to prevent the spread of the flu bacilli. (Years later, English doctors would discover that viruses caused influenza.)

The law was not popular. Men cut holes in the masks to smoke cigars and cigarettes. Women wore the masks as haremlike veils, hanging loose over the chin. Some cynics created masks with an extended snout, like a pig. Libertarians charged that the gauze was unconstitutional.

Citizens that ignored the ordinances risked a hundred dollar fine and thirty days in jail. But the police enforced the laws randomly and most of the 524 people arrested escaped with a five dollar fine.

Students at San Diego High School

Then, the flu disappeared as quickly and as mysteriously as it had arrived. After peaking in December, with 2,039 cases and 188 deaths in that month alone, the disease receded. According to city health officers, most of the credit was due to those 4-ply gauze masks.

135				Jail Register and Record of Arrest				
1918								
WHEN BROUGHT TO JAIL		NAME OF PRISONER	OFFENSE		ARRESTING OFFICER	AGE	OCCUPATION	
Dec 7	12:45 Pm	Fred Williams	Vio Flu Ord 7557		Buford-Wilson J.K	44	Engr	Amer
"	12:45 Pm	A. Gordalen	Vio Flu Ord "		Lankford	30	Lab	Mex
"	12:45 Pm	Jim Kelley	Drunk		Heise-Wilson J.K	49	Lab	Amer
"	1:00 am	Geo Contres	Vio Flu Ord 7557		Fay	37	Waiter	Grin
"	1:15 Pm	Gene DeRosa	Vio Flu Ord "		Heise	33	Waiter	Grin
"	1:15 Pm	G. N. Kattell	Vio Flu Ord "		Lankford	45	Agt	Amer
"	2:05 Pm	C. A. Dier	Vio Flu Ord "		Comstock	30	Druggist	Amer
"	2:15 Pm	Emmitt Myers	Deserter		Maj. Richards	28	Soldier	Amer
"	2:15 Pm	Juan Martis	Vio Flu Ord 7557		Heise	21	Lab	Mex
"	2:15 am	Jose Castro	Vio Flu Ord "		Heise	35	Lab	Mex
"	2:2 am	Harry Townsend	Vio Flu Ord "		Heise	40	Lab	Mex
"	2:30 am	Eg. Steans	Vio Flu Ord "		Lankford	29	Butcher	Amer
"	2:30 am	A. L. Scatterguod	Vio Flu Ord "		Irving	58	None	Fren
"	2:30 am	John A. Ferguson	Dis the Peace		Lopez-Carson	30	Saves	Cuba
"	2:45 Pm	Ramon R Rhodes	Vio Flu Ord 7557		Alvin-Heise	43	Black Smith	Amer

Citizens ignoring the flu ordinance could face arrest.

The S.S. Monte Carlo, *aground at Coronado.*

The Gambling Ships of San Diego

On a Saturday night in January 1936, the S.S. *Reno*, San Diego's first "floating pleasure palace," opened for business. Anchored three miles off Point Loma, the refurbished British Q-boat provided fine dining, dancing, and "sportive" games, described by the management as "ping-pong and other innocent pastimes." But a newspaper reporter observed that the ping pong tables were "curiously decorated with numbers from 1 to 36," and the "parchesi" boards had strange labels such as "come" and "don't come."

The gambling ship *Reno* was on instant hit with the sporting crowd of San Diego. Free water taxis ferried people daily try their luck at craps, roulette, blackjack, and poker. Local law enforcement officials found these games something less than innocent pastimes. District Attorney Thomas Whelan cited a State statute that prohibited the transport of people to gambling ships. Whelan tested the law by arresting one shore boat operator and several passengers. A Superior Court judge threw out the case, arguing that the statute was unconstitutional and furthermore, "the district attorney had no proof that gambling was conducted aboard the ship."

In April, the owners of the *Reno* decided to replace their ship with a larger vessel—the S.S. *Monte Carlo*. The new gambling ship was a rebuilt freighter—300 feet long with a concrete hull and no engines. As the *Monte Carlo* dropped anchor off Coronado, a tugboat returned the *Reno* to her home port of Long Beach.

Fun for the gamblers of San Diego lasted only a few more months. On December 31, a heavy winter storm hit Southern California. On board the *Monte Carlo*—closed for the winter since November 1—two caretakers awoke in the early morning to find that the anchor chain had snapped in the gale force winds. The men fired distress flares into the sky as they drifted helplessly toward shore. By daybreak the ship had grounded, broadside on the Coronado Strand. As ocean breakers pounded away at the *Monte Carlo's* wooden superstructure, a power launch from the Coast Guard cutter *Itasca* rescued the hapless caretakers.

Gambling paraphernalia littered the beach at Coronado.

Throughout the day, hundreds of people braved the wind and rain to watch the "Goddess of Chance" break up in the surf. Fashionably dressed vacationers from the nearby Hotel del Coronado waded through wet sand to scoop up roulette wheels, gambling tables, and other paraphernalia that littered the beach for hundreds of yards. The crowd became especially attentive to the debris after a rumor circulated that hundreds of cases of whiskey remained on board. Representatives of the ship scotched the story but not before a sailor drowned while trying to swim to the wreck.

In the days that followed, efforts to salvage the *Monte Carlo* proved futile. After a few articles were removed from the wreck via an overhead tram, the owners surrendered the hulk to the waves. For more than a decade the battered casino ship remained visible to beachgoers. As late as the winter of 1975, the ship's rudder was exposed at low tide—a rusty reminder of San Diego's brief flirtation with legalized gambling.

The San Diego & Escondido Stage Line, circa 1906.

Stagecoach Days

Our stages were the Concord type, miserable things to ride in. The motion made the passengers sea-sick, and the dust was terrible.

—Katie Leng, stagecoach passenger.

Stagecoach travel was no picnic in backcountry San Diego of the 1800s, but until the appearance of automobiles on county roads after the turn of the century, travelers had little choice in their mode of travel. Horse-drawn coaches offered reliable service—albeit slow, dusty, bumpy, and occasionally, eventful.

Stagecoaches first appeared in the San Diego region in 1852 with the establishment of erratic service between San Diego and Los Angeles. The route required two full days of travel.

By the 1860s, the Seeley & Wright stage line boasted of regular service to Los Angeles, three times a week, on the "very best Concord Stages." The stages left Old Town at 5:00 AM and finished the day at San Juan Capistrano by 7:00 PM. Arrival in Los Angeles came at 4:00 PM the next day.

Although two-day journeys were the norm, some drivers claimed faster transits. A veteran of the coast route was driver Don Luis Serrano. In 1933, at age 87, Serrano recalled driving the coast route:

Frank Shaw and I were the drivers for Seeley's stages. We left at seven a.m., one from here and the other from Los Angeles; the distance was 145 miles. We drove four horse Concord stages.... The trip took twelve hours. The horses were tough mustangs, about half-broken, and as soon as they were hitched we were off on a run. Shaw and I would meet at San Luis Rey, and always saluted each other with a vigorous crack of our whips. I drove two years without an accident, due no doubt to the efficacy of prayer.

As San Diego County grew, other stage lines flourished. In 1858, the famed Butterfield Overland Mail route crossed the Southwest from St. Louis, Missouri to Los Angeles enroute to San Francisco. Bypassing the city of San Diego, the route covered much of northern San Diego county. Traveling northwest from Yuma on the way to Los Angeles, the Butterfield stage passed through Vallecito, the San Felipe Valley, Warner Ranch, and Oak Grove. (Today, these restored historic sites are designated as official San Diego County landmarks.)

Several San Diego stage lines served the northern county until about 1912. The well-traveled San Diego-Escondido stage route was recalled by Daisy Abell, the husband of a stage driver, in 1961:

> There were just old dirt roads then [1890s] and it took eight hours to make the trip between San Diego and Escondido. The stages ran every day—one would leave San Diego and one would leave Escondido at eight o'clock in the morning.

Poway was the half-way station, commonly called the "Twenty-mile house." "The stages had four horse teams," remembered Daisy, "and were Concord stages with several seats, built like a ship with leather straps for [springs]." Later, flat bed stages would replace some of the Concord wagons.

Stage lines also ran from San Diego to the booming mining camps of Julian and Banner. The San Diego Cuyamaca Railroad shortened the distance to the mines in 1895. Running twice a day from San Diego, passenger trains dropped off travelers to the north county at Foster Station east of El Cajon. The stage

STAGE LINE,

BETWEEN

San Diego and **Los Angeles,**

CALIFORNIA.

LEAVES the Franklin House in San Diego, every Monday, Wednesday and Friday, at 5 o'clock A. M., arriving at San Juan Capistrano at 7 o'clock P. M., and remaining there over night, and reaching Los Angeles the following day at 4 o'clock P. M.

Leaves Bella Union Hotel in Los Angeles every Monday, Wednesday and Friday at 8 o'clock A. M., arriving at San Juan Capistrano at 5 o'clock P. M., and remaining there over night reaches San Diego at 6½ o'clock.

This line of Stages passes through

San Diegita,

Encinitos,

San Luis Rey,

Los Flores,

San Juan Capistrano,

Anaheim,

Los Nietos,

The best part of Southern California. Persons wishing to see the country should not fail to make this trip.

THE VERY BEST

Concord Stages

run on this line, and the STOOK cannot be excelled or any stage line on the Pacific slope.

STAGE OFFICE—At the Franklin Hotel, San Diego.

SEELEY & WRIGHT,

may19:tf   Proprietors.

would set off from Foster at ten in the morning, arriving first in Ramona where passengers had dinner, then on to Ballena for a change of horses. The stagecoach passed through Santa Ysabel then on to Julian after a ten hour journey.

Bad roads and harsh weather often made the Julian stage run an exciting experience. The *San Diego Union* reported a typical incident in February 1883.

> Frank Frary, who drove the Julian stage in last evening, says that when he started yesterday morning the wind was blowing a perfect hurricane from the east and northeast. The stage swayed so violently in the gale, that fearful that it would capsize, he and the two passengers piled two or three hundred pounds of rocks into the vehicle as ballast, which they carried until the grade had been passed.

Katie Leng, the niece of Julian stage operator, Joe Foster, recalled the stages were "miserable things to ride in." In an interview in 1972 for the San Diego Historical Society, Leng offered the last word on stagecoach travel:

The stagecoach at the Ramona Hotel, circa 1900

> Let me say that the stage coaches galloping along in the Western movies always upsets me, because is wasn't that way at all. The horses were trotted, with frequent breathers.... Also, there was only one man on the box, and I never knew of any of them being armed. They wore any sort of clothing they wanted to; nothing flamboyant. We never had a hold-up. The only real tragedy I ever heard of was once, before my time, a driver was leading his team across a usually dry wash and was caught by a flash flood and drowned.

[A restored Concord stagecoach can be viewed at Museum of San Diego History in Balboa Park. The Frary and Foster stagecoach was brought to San Diego in 1886 by Joe Foster and used on the El Cajon to Julian run until 1910.]

A Case of Discrimination

In the 1890s, the people of San Diego believed that the finest theater west of Chicago could be found at the Fisher Opera House on 4th Street. Throughout the decade, glittering productions drew sell-out crowds to the majestic Romanesque style edifice. However, not all San Diegans were permitted to enjoy the local theater. In 1897, the popular playhouse was the scene of an ugly incident of discrimination.

On May 17, a young black businessman named Edward W. Anderson bought two tickets to a production of "Around the World in Eighty Days." When Anderson and his wife Mary arrived at the Opera House that night the doorkeeper admitted them to the foyer but refused to allow them to take their seats in the orchestra circle. Claiming that the seats were already occupied, the doorkeeper told the couple that duplicate tickets had been sold by mistake.

John C. Fisher, the theater's builder and manager, stepped forward and pointed to a disclaimer printed on the back of the Anderson's tickets: "The right reserved to refuse admission to holder of this ticket by return of money." Fisher announced that he was exercising his right to refuse admission,

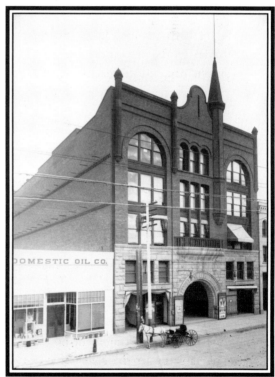

The Fisher Opera House

adding, "furthermore I do not allow colored people on that floor." Taking the refund, the Anderson's left the theater and ignored Fisher's offer to let them stand at the rear of the balcony.

Edward and Mary Anderson decided to sue for damages. John C. Fisher would not be easy to defeat in court. The ambitious promoter, entrepreneur, and former president of the Chamber of Commerce, was popular in the community as the man who had brought large-scale entertainment to San Diego. But the law clearly addressed the Andersons' charges. A California civil rights act, passed only weeks previously, prohibited public houses from discriminating on the basis of race or color. "Anderson vs. Fisher" would serve as an important test case for this significant legislative act.

In justice court, judge Solon Bryan found that under the new law he had "no alternative" but to decide in favor of the plaintiffs. Bryan awarded the Andersons a judgement of $150. Fisher immediately appealed to Superior Court. There, the Anderson case foundered. Judge E. S. Torrance held that the plaintiffs had not been damaged to a degree sufficient to give his court jurisdiction. He ordered the case dismissed.

The ornate interior of the Opera House

The Andersons successfully appealed for another hearing. In the new trial Fisher argued that his theater was not a public entertainment house but rather a "private enterprise" and therefore not liable under the civil rights act. Without commenting on this unique assertion, Judge Torrance once again rejected the case. Moreover, he ordered the plaintiffs to pay for the costs of the suit.

In the fall of 1899, the state Supreme Court declined to listen to a final appeal. After nearly three years of fruitless litigation, the Andersons had exhausted all legal avenues and a case of overt racial discrimination had been upheld in the courts of California.

The Englishman at Rincon

"P.S. SPARKMAN MURDERED AT RINCON"
"WELL KNOWN MERCHANT FOUND
WITH BULLET IN HEAD BY INDIAN"

In bold headlines the San Diego newspapers of May 21, 1907, announced a shocking crime: the murder of Philip Stedman Sparkman, a storekeeper in the small community of Rincon, at the foot of Mt. Palomar.

Sparkman was a popular man and known throughout San Diego County. But to most of his friends and acquaintances, Sparkman was an enigma. Only in death did San Diego learn that the quiet bachelor, "the Englishman at Rincon," was actually an accomplished scholar who would leave important academic contributions to his region.

Philip Stedman Sparkman

Sparkman came to America at age nineteen, sailing from Liverpool with £50 in his pocket. Slowly making his way west, he found work in railroad yards of Albuquerque, New Mexico. He decided the way to get ahead in the West was to become a merchant, and in 1880, he opened a store in Albuquerque. But more moves followed. After several short-lived store ventures in the rough towns along the Santa Fe Trail, Sparkman decided to go to California, "resolving never to go into business in a town again."

Rincon, with a small population of ranchers and Indians, was what Sparkman had waited for. For the next eighteen years he prospered in the quiet, rural community. His well-stocked store and honest business habits made him a respected member of his community. A friend noted that Sparkman lived simply in an adobe house only thirty yards from his store. He was "very neat and methodical, quiet, studious...even tempered...temperate in his habits, not even using tobacco." A neighbor, rancher Louis Salmons, recalled:

This Sparkman was an Englishman. When you've said that you've said a lot. He was a very peculiar man. You'd walk in the store, and he'd stand there with his hand on the counter and wait for you to pick out something. He was a fine man. I knew him better than anyone around here.

But to Salmons and other friends who thought they knew him, Philip Sparkman was simply a country storekeeper, albeit a strangely bookish storekeeper with an intense curiosity in the local Indians, the Luiseños.

Sparkman found the Indians fascinating. Before coming to San Diego County, the merchant had taught himself Spanish while living in New Mexico. Now, he decided to learn the Luiseño language and culture. It began as a hobby, soon it became an obsession.

He built two rooms behind his store: a spare bedroom, and a study where he could retreat in leisure moments to "puzzle out the idioms and construction of the language." He hired an Indian boy named Gomez to come to the store in the evenings to teach him the tongue, word for word. The old men of the tribe provided more words and meanings, and told Sparkman of their ancient customs and rituals.

For years, Sparkman spent every spare moment recording all facets of the Luiseño culture—their folklore, customs, religion, and, most importantly, their complex language. Eventually, he mastered the difficult vocabulary, and for the first time, the previously unwritten Luiseño speech was recorded in text. A neatly typed manuscript was bound into volumes.

Late Sunday night, May 19th, Sparkman was shot and killed in the yard in front of his store. His body was found early the next morning. Although a light still burned brightly in the store, nothing was missing. The authorities surmised that Sparkman had been lured from his house late at night, probably by someone he knew. There had been no robbery, no explanation for the murder. He was fifty years old.

The newspapers quickly blamed Indians for the crime but no arrests were made. It would have been ironic, and certainly unlikely, for Philip Sparkman to have been killed by a Native American. A coroner's jury closed the case after a few days, ruling that Sparkman had died from wounds inflicted by parties unknown.

One week after the murder, Edward H. Davis, a friend of Sparkman's from Mesa Grande, revealed in the *San Diego Union* the story of the storekeeper's work recording the language and customs of the Luiseño Indians. "His monumental work on their language," wrote Davis, "is of the highest and most scientific order of any that has ever been written in this country."

The next year, Philip Sparkman's *Culture of the Luiseño Indians* was published by

IN THE SUPERIOR COURT OF THE COUNTY OF SAN DIEGO,

STATE OF CALIFORNIA.

————:::::————

In the Matter of the Estate)

    -of-)

PHILIP S. SPARKMAN,)   No. 3504. Dept. 2.

      Deceased.) INVENTORY of STOCK of MERCHAN-
               DISE in Store at Rincon, said
               County.

————:::::————

STORE ROOM NEAR DOOR:-

47	heel taps,	25
14	oz. Capewell horse nails,	15
2-1/2 lbs.	No. 6 horse nails,	50
5 lbs.	No.7 horse nails,	1 00
9	6-in. lbl. bolts,	50
1/2 box cigars,		
40	packages cigarettes,papers,	20
	packages "Dixie Queen" tobacco,	40
11	" "C.C "	33
8	" "Creole" tobacco,	
13	" "Duke's Mixture"tobacco,	40
34	" "Bull Durham" "	2 50
3 packages Gloss starch,		20
6	" Corn "	30
2	" "Arm and Hammer" Soda,	10
1	jar spice,	75
6	doz. jar-rubbers,	15
1	gross "Perfection" jar-rubbers,	60
2	jars mustard,	20
4	cans "	20
8	bottles pepper sauce,	50
7	cans sage,	50
5	cans ginger,	35

-1-   To.08

An inventory page from the probate case of Philip Sparkman

the University of California. His monumental *Grammar and Dictionary* of the Luiseño language was also published. Both classics of anthropology, the remarkable works of the modest English storekeeper are respected to this day.

The Smallpox Fear of 1862-63

We are all badly scared by the smallpox. We keep a sentinel posted to give notice of the approach of anyone and we have to know about them before they can come nearer to the corral . . .Many have done the same thing. I have stopped my vaqueros in their rounds...

—Cave Johnson Couts, San Luis Rey, 1862.

For much of the nineteenth century the scourge of smallpox frightened frontier communities in the United States. Despite the existence of effective vaccines, epidemics of the deadly disease often wreaked havoc, particularly among Mexicans and Native Americans. An outbreak of smallpox in 1862 killed hundreds in Southern California, many in San Diego County.

Cave J. Couts, a successful cattleman from Rancho Guajome at San Luis Rey, proved to be the best chronicler of the outbreak. "Small pox is quite prevalent," wrote Couts to a friend, "six to eight per day are being buried in S.Juan Capistrano—Indians generally." Many victims were buried in the *campo santo* of Mission San Luis Rey, where, Couts observed, "a grave cannot be dug without striking human bone...they [Indians] were digging little holes, barely enough to cover their coffins...."

Cave J. Couts

The cemetery at Mission San Luis Rey would be the scene of a tragic incident on January 13, 1863, when family and friends came to bury smallpox victim Don Ysidro María Alvarado, a well known cattleman from Rancho Monserrate, a few miles northeast of San Luis Rey. As Cave Couts would report the next day: "In avoiding the loathsome disease now infesting our community, we have had to resort to arms, resulting in the killing of one man."

The prominence of Alvarado had not swayed fellow rancher Cave Couts from deciding there would be no more burials of smallpox victims at the mission, a property he owned. Hearing that Don Ysidro was about to be buried, he dispatched his younger brother, William Blount Couts, to stop the burial. Blount, along with two servants, arrived at the cemetery in a carriage. Alvarado's son, Tomãs, remembered what followed:

The cemetery at Mission San Luis Rey

Being inside the graveyard, we lowered the coffin into the grave. We were throwing the first earth over the coffin, when Blunt Couts arrived, suddenly, without our looking or thinking of him, and came close to the wall [of the graveyard], and said, '*Como diputado del Sherif del condado, no es permitido que este Señor se entierra aqui.*' [As deputy of the sheriff of the county, you are not permitted to bury this man here.] At the time he said this, he had in his hands a gun of two barrels.

One member of the burial party, Leon Vasquez, was outraged by the presence of Couts. With a shovel in his hand, the vaquero impulsively rushed toward Couts, who fired one barrel in Vasquez's direction. As Vasquez jumped up on the wall of the *campo santo*, Couts fired his second barrel. Struck in the face, Vasquez slumped over the wall, dead.

The unarmed burial party scattered in fear. Couts' servant, Miguel, fired more shots, wounding two men. "The whole affair was the act of a moment," recalled Tomãs, "the shots and death— all was *muy pronto.*"

In a letter to his attorney, Blount's brother, Cave, defended the action by saying, "the fellow killed is really not worth noticing...He (Vasquez) is known as a bad character."

Three months later, a county justice of the peace indicted William Blount Couts on a charge of murder. Couts' attorney, citing a variety of problems in the indictment paperwork, succeeded in having the charge dropped, despite depositions from eight eyewitnesses.

Meanwhile, the smallpox epidemic had run its course. By the spring of 1863, the disease, and the fear, had passed.

Pride of the West Mine, Julian, 1900

Gold Fever

While few people know Southern California for its mineral wealth, San Diego County—from the Laguna Mountains in the east to the foothills of Escondido—has contributed millions of dollars in gold to the Golden State.

San Diego's best known mining period—the Julian gold rush of 1870—began when rancher Fred Coleman spotted gold in a creek in the Cuyamaca Mountains.

When Coleman spread word of his discovery, scores of prospectors raced to the hills to pan for placer gold in the mountain streams. The miners formed a mining district, and a town of tents emerged called Emily City.

In San Diego, skepticism over the strike vanished when a load of 1,500 pounds of gold ore arrived in town in March, 1870. The *San Diego Union* reported the event:

> The arrival of so large a quantity of rich gold-bearing quartz created intense excitement in town. A stampede immediately ensued and the road has now for several days been lined with teams of every description and men mounted and on foot in route to the mines. From persons who returned yesterday we learned that there are now on the ground not less than 600 persons and the number is daily increasing.

Julian gold fever soon infected the whole of the Southwest. Miners poured into the region from San Francisco via steamer or overland from Los Angeles.

The miners found lode gold in several hillside areas. The claims bore formal names such as George Washington, Mount Vernon, The Monroe, and U.S. Grant, as well as novel titles such as Shoo Fly, April Fool, You Bet, and Don't Bother Me.

The first significant town site was laid out by homesteader Drury Bailey and named "Julian City" after his cousin, Mike Julian. A tent city at first, Julian grew in two years to a population of nearly 2,000—half the size of San Diego. At its gold-rush peak, the town boasted two hotels, two cafes, five stores, two blacksmith shops, two livery stables, a school, a race track, and uncounted saloons and dance halls. The town became important politically after Mike Julian was appointed county assessor. (An attempt to move the county seat to Julian from San Diego failed.)

Neighboring mining camps grew up in the region: Branson City, Eastwood, and Coleman City (Emily City). Banner, located a few miles southwest of Julian, became a sizeable town.

The mining boom of Julian-Banner lasted fewer than five years. In 1873 the camps produced $500,000 in gold, but late in the year, plans for the long- anticipated Texas and Pacific Railroad collapsed. A severe recession gripped the region. Gold production began to decline and, by 1876, most of the mines had closed. The population of Julian fell to under one hundred people, and Banner became a ghost town. Between 1870 and 1875 the mines had produced about $2 million in gold.

The late 1800s saw a major revival in mining, helped by the completion of railroad connections to the north. The new rail and stage lines promoted fresh interest in mining ventures. The most successful activity came from the Stonewall

Miners at the Helvetia Mine of Julian, 1901

Mine south of Julian. Purchased by California Governor Robert W. Waterman for $75,000, the mine yielded $1 million in gold between 1888 and 1891.

Gold mining was not confined to the mountains of the northeast county. In the 1890s, prospectors found gold in the Escondido region. The Cleveland-Pacific, Oro Fino, and Cravath mines, located only two miles southeast of the Escondido city hall, produced about $150,000 (at $20 per ounce) in the early century.

The Cleveland-Pacific Mining Company developed the most important site from 1896 through 1911. A 350-foot incline shaft followed a vein of gold-bearing quartz. Ore was processed at the site using a five-stamp mill and 10-foot high tanks of cyanide. Slow activity continued from the 1920s until about 1932, when all mining stopped and the shafts were dynamited shut. Citrus and avocado groves soon covered all traces of the mines.

Reminders of the San Diego County gold producing days still exist, though. Old mine dumps near the junction of San Pasqual Valley Road and Bear Valley Parkway can be seen today as low hills. The site of the Stonewall Mine near the southeast shore of Cuyamaca Reservoir is clearly marked within Cuyamaca State Park and easily reached by visitors. The Eagle-High Peak Mine of Julian produces gold to this day and even provides guided tours of the diggings.

When San Diego Went Dry

On the eve of Prohibition, the *San Diego Sun* ran an obituary on the front page:

DEATHS

BARLEYCORN in this city June 30, 1919. John B. Corn beloved great grand daddy of Old Mick Redeye, and Aching Head; a native of the Garden of Eden, age 5041 years, 27 days, 11 hours, 2 minutes. Friends and victims are invited to attend the funeral services tonight at midnight. Please omit flowers.

The demise of Mr. Barleycorn was occasioned by the federal War Prohibition Act which outlawed the sale of intoxicating beverages. Passed only days after the end of World War I, the law was scheduled to take effect on July 1, only six months before the effective date of the Eighteenth Amendment (Volstead Act). California would finally go "dry" and join thirty-three other states that already thirsted under prohibition laws.

San Diegans had no intention of facing the coming drought without one last blowout. After a plea from banker Joseph Sefton, representing local business interests, the city council voted unanimously to temporarily suspend an ordinance that stopped liquor sales after 6:00 P.M. For one night only, revelers would be allowed to buy liquor until midnight.

The police braced themselves for an early New Year's party. Double shifts were added including the detective force, plainclothesmen, and the entire clerical staff. Police court judge W. F. Schuermeyer announced his schedule of fines for public drunkenness and the city jail was whipped into shape for an expected full house.

That night, from dusk until midnight, drinkers mobbed the city's fifty-five saloons. Customers stood three and four deep at most bars. The liquor stores were even more chaotic as people grabbed their last opportunity to stock up. Some store owners even raised prices as brisk sales emptied their shelves. As midnight approached, "the last trickles of booze burst into belligerency." But the police tolerated most of the "fistic encounters" and made fewer than thirty arrests.

The next day downtown streets showed the evidence of the late celebration. Broken whiskey bottles littered the sidewalks and the odor of stale beer filled the air. A reporter for the *Sun* observed that "Old Sol, creeping over the Cuyamacas

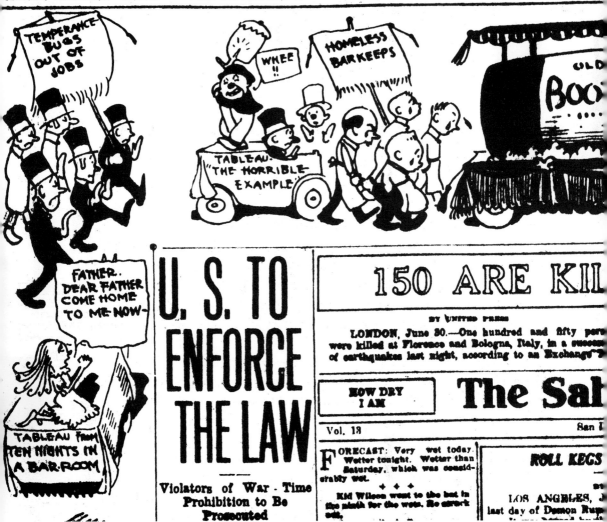

this morning, found more splitting headaches and coated tongues" than any time since Cabrillo.

For the next fourteen years San Diego remained "dry." More or less. Nearby Tijuana stayed "wet" and rum runners on the coast could always supply liquor for a price. Repeal of Prohibition finally came in December 1933. And San Diego had another party.

30, 1919

D IN QUAKE

dispatch from Rome today. At Vecchinea, Italy, 100
a were killed, the dispatch said. It added that several
persons were injured in the three cities. The
shocks continued throughout the night.

Signal

GOODBYE TO LICKER

day   Price: A Memory

K IN L. A.

eration marked the
county
camels from a movie
the normal drink for
hat the camels would

the number of arrests, says Police
Chief Patrick. He figures that the
reserve stock is so widely distrib
uted and so plentiful that it will
continue to furnish the police
court with drunk cases for at least
half a year

◆ ◆ ◆

Among other things which the
demise of John B. Corn will bring
is suppression of the abused pest
who insists on reciting "The Face

GOODBYE TO KING ALCOHOL

City Bids It Farewell To
night; Predict Scenes
of Revelry

PRAYNO

The Tumor Mania

It is an open question whether there is a community on the Pacific coast so easily swindled.

Thus did the San Francisco *Chronicle* mock the red-faced citizens of San Diego, the apparent victims of "tumor mania," in the summer of 1882.

The mania involved Mrs. Lou Patterson, alias Dr. Patterson, "a large, coarse woman," known in San Diego as a spiritualist. As a medium she conducted seances and gave spiritualist lectures while in a "trance state." She claimed a wide following and became particularly popular among bereaved people who had recently lost relatives, friends, or loved ones in death. Her true talents, however, lay in the field of medicine.

The doctor took special interest in her female followers. If she found that a woman was in any manner "indisposed" she had a ready diagnosis: "the patient was afflicted with a tumor in a private part, which she (the doctor) could remove without loss of blood or danger to life." The spiritual doctress charged seventy-five dollars for this procedure, payable in advance.

Dr. Patterson's surgical practice boomed, unhindered by the lack of any known medical degree. One housewife after another submitted to the miraculous, blood-less operation. Husbands paid the bills without complaint. Many of the patients were wives or daughters of San Diego's social or political elite: E. W. Bushyhead, publisher of the *Union*; Sylvester Statler, the County Clerk; Thomas Bush, a former county Judge; and Jesse A. Shepherd, the assistant to Alonzo Horton.

The doctor preserved the extracted tumors in bottles which she presented to her patients. "It was a common fashion among the women," reported the *Chronicle*, "to exhibit to one another the tumors that Mrs. Patterson had removed from them, as children do their dolls when they go visiting." One satisfied customer reportedly paid to have nineteen tumors removed in the span of three days.

But one skeptical husband was reluctant to spend seventy-five dollars on his wife's prescribed surgery.

In order to convince him... an original, live tumor, which the doctress had but recently taken from a lady without loss of blood, was procured. He thereupon took this original and wonderful tumor to his family physician. Upon examination, the physician had some doubts about the tumor qualities of the thing presented.

[*San Diego Sun*]

Seven doctors in all, ruled the object a pig's kidney, "such as ordinarily used for a hotel stew." Another tumor they examined seemed to be a combination of kidney, liver, and the windpipe of a chicken. The organs had been cooked, making exact identification difficult.

A criminal complaint was filed on behalf of Miss Mary J. McClelland, a recent patient. Mrs. Patterson was arrested at her Sherman Heights home and arraigned in justice court on a felony charge of "obtaining money under false pretenses." Before a packed hearing room, Justice Joseph Leonard ordered the case bound over to Superior Court.

Wm. Jeff Gatewood

In the next several days, prosecutor W. Jeff Gatewood paraded a dozen embarrassed victims before an all-male jury and a fascinated audience in the hearing room of Superior Court. The women testified that Mrs. Patterson had diagnosed their ailments by examining locks of their hair and then performed surgery while in a "spiritual trance." When Patterson herself took the stand she admitted to a prior conviction in San Francisco for practicing medicine without a license.

THE TUMOR MANIA.

Work of a San Diego Spiritualist Impostor

WHO COUNTED HER DUPES BY SCORES.

Women Relieved of Tumors Which Were Proved to Be Pig's Kidneys—A Gross and Filthy Fraud.

[Correspondence of the CHRONICLE.]
SAN DIEGO, July 25, 1882.

The denizens of this ambitious city are wont to pride themselves on their enterprise and pluck. They even plume themselves on their sharpness, but it is an open question whether there is a community on the Pacific coast so easily swindled. It is hardly possible to conceive of a more astounding or outrageous imposition than has been practiced in this community by a woman during the past four months. About six or eight months ago a Mrs. Patterson, a large, coarse woman, came here and set up as a Spiritualist doctor. She made no stir in the community, until, from the Spiritualists here, she had informed herself about many of the families of this place. She then blossomed out into a medium, and, associated with a Mrs. Seal, gave Spiritualistic lectures while in a trance state and went through the fraudulent performances usual with the professional Spiritualists. With much cunning she selected as her first victims those who had recently lost near relatives, husbands, wives or children, by death. A number of mothers who had lost children and were mourning and despondent, fell easy victims to her wiles.

SPREAD OF THE DELUSION.

When she had apparently got these entirely under her control, through them she reached out for all classes, and a genuine mania ensued. Steady-going business men, church members, even real estate dealers, became converts. The regular medical faculty took

San Francisco Chronicle, *28 July 1882*

After deliberating only forty minutes, the jury returned a verdict of guilty. Judge W. T. McNealy sentenced Mrs. Patterson to a term of six months in the county jail and a fine of $250.

Within ten days the "tumor fiend" was free on a writ of habeas corpus. Her case was transferred to the Superior Court of Los Angeles where she was soon released, the court deciding it had "no jurisdiction over matters supernatural." At last report Dr. Patterson was promoting herself in Los Angeles newspapers as a clairvoyant and medium. Her advertisements read: "Tumors removed at reduced rates."

The Last of the Narwhal

A ship without a country,
A mast without a sail.
Then someone swiped the galley range,
And that's the *Narwhal's* tale!

These were the words of newspaper reporter (later director of the San Diego Historical Society) Jerry MacMullen in the fall of 1932 as the storied whaling ship *Narwhal* was towed to the mudflats off National City and abandoned. In earlier days the steam bark *Narwhal* had been the prize of the San Francisco whaling fleet as it hunted bowhead whales in the North Pacific and Arctic Ocean. Later, the ship's career would end in ignominy in San Diego Bay.

Launched in 1883, the *Narwhal* made seventeen voyages to the Arctic for the Pacific Steam Whaling Company. Whaling was big business in the late 1800s. Whalebone corsets were the rage and a single bowhead whale contained thousands of dollars worth of "corset stays in the rough." But women's fashion changed, spring steel replaced whalebone for most uses, and the industry declined. The *Narwhal* was retired from whaling in 1908 after the longest and most successful career of any steam whaler.

For the next several years the ship served as a salmon packer—a fate shared by other old barks including the *Star of India*. In 1926, the *Narwhal* went into the movies, starring in a Warner Brothers version of "Moby Dick" called "The Sea Beast." Bit parts followed until she was sold to Mexico for use as a fishing barge.

Anchored off Ensenada in February, 1932, the *Narwhal* became known as a "ghost ship." A caretaker hired to watch the ship lasted just one day after a night of strange noises—"a hand-power foghorn, beating on the deck, wild yells" and, worst of all, "phantasmal shapes flitting around the deserted decks." After the *Narwhal* dragged her anchors, nearly destroying Ensenada's best pier, a tugboat hooked on and towed the ship to San Diego.

The *Narwhal* was docked at the pier of the San Diego Marine Construction Company. Her ownership uncertain, the leaky ship became the target of scavengers:

Narwhal, *abandoned on the beach off National City, 1932. Courtesy San Diego Maritime Museum Association.*

Men and boys with skiffs, wrenches, screwdrivers, knives and crowbars were awake to the situation. In short order she was stripped to a gantline—and then they stole the gantline. They took the brass rims from her portlights; they cut away her lifts and braces; they walked off with the wheel, and the doors and the companion-ladders. They even stole the galley range.

Finally, in October, the old ship was pumped out, towed away and beached at National City. When port director Joe Brennan decided that the hulk was a menace to navigation and "the morals of the young," a wrecker was hired to tear up the ship and remove the remains. For unknown reasons the work was never done. Slowly, over time, the *Narwhal* fell to pieces in the wind and surf.

One more chapter to the *Narwhal* saga remained. On the night of August 24, 1937, a Navy seaplane from North Island came in for a landing on the water of the South Bay. Suddenly, the plane hit an obstruction, nosed over and sank in eight feet of water. Six fliers were killed in the crash, two more were injured. "About twenty yards away," wrote MacMullen, "looming starkly black and looking like the gaunt skeleton of some primeval sea beast, was the hull of the *Narwhal*."

Narwhal *docked in San Diego harbor. Courtesy San Diego Maritime Museum Association*

For Further Reading

THE "LOST" TREASURE OF FRANCISCO DE ULLOA

Clausen, Genevieve. "The Remarkable Dr. Markey." *San Diego Magazine* 23 (June 1971); (August 1971).

Garrahy, Stephen T. and David J. Weber. "Francisco de Ulloa, Joseph James Markey, and the Discovery of Upper California." *California Historical Society Quarterly* 50 (March 1971).

"Oceanside Archaeology," Vertical File. Heritage Room, Oceanside Public Library.

Wagner, Henry Raup. "Francisco de Ulloa Returned." *California Historical Society Quarterly* 19 (September 1940).

THE PEOPLE VS. CAVE J. COUTS

Porter, Rufus K., *Letters to the San Francisco Bulletin*, October 1866.

San Diego County, County Court. "People of the State of California vs. Cave J. Couts." Case no. 174. Research Archives, San Diego Historical Society.

San Diego County, Office of Coroner. Coroner's Inquests, 1853-1905. Research Archives, San Diego Historical Society.

THE GOLD OF HEDGES

San Diego County, Superior Court. "Golden Cross Mining and Milling Company vs. James Speirs, et al." Case no. 10,215. Research Archives, San Diego Historical Society.

San Diego Union, 1894-1905.

Van Wormer, Stephen R. and James D. Newland. "Hedges and the Cargo Muchacho Mining District: A Case Study of Mexican Mineros and Corporate Mining in the Southern California Desert." *Journal of San Diego History.* (forthcoming.)

THE WHALEMEN OF SAN DIEGO BAY

May, Ronald V. "Dog-Holes, Bomb-Lances and Devil-Fish: Boom Times for the San Diego Whaling Industry." *Journal of San Diego History* 32 (Spring 1986): 72-91.

Scammon, Charles M. *The Marine Mammals of the Northwestern Coast of North America.* San Francisco: John H. Carmany and Co., 1874; reprint, New York: Dover Publications, Inc., 1968.

FRANK BUCK IN SAN DIEGO

San Diego County, Superior Court. "Frank H. Buck vs. Zoological Society of San Diego, a Corporation, and Harry M. Wegeforth." Case no. 40,507. County Clerk, County of San Diego.

Wegeforth, Harry Milton, M.D. and Neil Morgan, *It Began With a Roar: the Story of San Diego's World-Famed Zoo.* San Diego: Pioneer Printers, 1953.

"IT'S THE WATER"

The Golden Era. May 1887, October 1887.

Howard-Jones, Marje. *Seekers of the Spring: A History of Carlsbad.* Carlsbad, Calif.: Friends of the Carlsbad Public Library, 1982.

Union Title-Trust Topics. July-August 1949.

THE "REAL" RAMONA

Brigandi, Phil and John W. Robinson. "The Killing of Juan Diego: From Murder to Mythology." *Journal of San Diego History* 40 (Winter/Spring 1994).

Jackson, Helen Hunt. *A Century of Dishonor.* Boston: Roberts Brother, 1886.

"Jackson, Helen Hunt," Documents File. Research Archives, San Diego Historical Society.

San Diego County, Justice Court, San Jacinto Township.

"People of the State of California vs. Samuel Temple." 31 March 1883. Research Archives, San Diego Historical Society.

FRONTIER SAN DIEGO: THE LETTERS OF THOMAS DARNALL

Thomas Ryland Darnall Collection. Research Archives, San Diego Historical Society.

THE RENEGADE REPUBLICAN

Higgins, Shelley J. *This Fantastic City.* San Diego: City of San Diego, 1956.

Smythe, William E. *History of San Diego, 1542-1908.* San Diego: The History Company, 1908.

THE GREAT DROUGHT

Cleland, Robert Glass. *The Cattle on a Thousand Hills: Southern California, 1850-1870.* San Marino, Calif.: The Huntington Library, 1941.

Hayes, Benjamin. *Pioneer Notes from the Diaries of Judge Benjamin Hayes, 1849-1875.* Los Angeles, 1929.

Pourade, Richard F. *The Silver Dons.* San Diego: Union-Tribune Publishing Company, 1963.

Smythe, William E. *History of San Diego, 1542-1908.* San Diego: The History Company, 1908.

DEADMAN'S HOLE

"Deadman's Hole," Vertical File. Research Archives, San Diego Historical Society.

San Diego County, Office of Coroner. Coroner's Inquests, 1853-1905. Research Archives, San Diego Historical Society.

VIGILANTE JUSTICE

San Diego County, District Court. Case files, 1850-1880. Research Archives, San Diego Historical Society.

San Diego County, Office of Coroner. Coroner's Inquests, 1853-1905. Research Archives, San Diego Historical Society.

Smythe, William E. *History of San Diego, 1542-1908.* San Diego: The History Company, 1908.

FRONTIER MEDICINE

Gaskill, Luman H. "Book of Records, Campo." Research Archives, San Diego Historical Society.

MacKechnie, Lois Gaskill. Interview by Bob Wright, 8 October 1972. Research Archives, San Diego Historical Society.

THE MYSTERIOUS DEATH OF OLEGARIO

County of San Diego, Board of Supervisors. "Petition Filed with County Board of Supervisors Protesting the Exhumation and Inquest on the Body of Olegario, an Indian." (1877) Research Archives, San Diego Historical Society.

San Diego Union. November 1871, October-November 1875, June-August 1877.

THE SPANISH FLU

Stickney, Jefferson K., Jr. "S.A.T.C.: San Diego's Student Army." *Journal of San Diego History* 27 (Summer 1981).

San Diego Union. November-December 1918.

THE GAMBLING SHIPS OF SAN DIEGO

San Diego Sun. December 1936.

San Diego Union. December 1936, January 1937

STAGECOACH DAYS

Abell, Daisy Harbin. Interview by Edgar F. Hastings, 20 January 1961. Research Archives, San Diego Historical Society.

Leng, Katherine N. Interview by Bob Wright, 30 July 1972. Research Archives, San Diego Historical Society.

Virden, Bill. "The Concord Stage." *Journal of San Diego History* 8 (January 1962).

A CASE OF DISCRIMINATION

San Diego County, Superior Court. "E. Anderson vs. John C. Fisher." Case no. 10,274. Research Archives, San Diego Historical Society.

San Diego Union. 17 August 1897, 24 February 1899

THE ENGLISHMAN AT RINCON

Thornburgh, Margaret. "The Englishman at Rincon." *Westways* (September 1954).

San Diego County, Probate Court. Case no. 3504. Research Archives, San Diego Historical Society.

San Diego Union. May 1907.

THE SMALLPOX FEAR OF 1862

Hayes, Benjamin. *Pioneer Notes from the Diaries of Judge Benjamin Hayes, 1849-1875.* Los Angeles, 1929.

Pourade, Richard F. *The Silver Dons.* San Diego: Union-Tribune Publishing Company, 1963.

San Diego County, County Court. "People of the State of California vs. W. B. Couts." Case no. 174B. Research Archives, San Diego Historical Society.

GOLD FEVER

Cleveland-Pacific Mining Company Collection. Research Archives, San Diego Historical Society.

Pourade, Richard F. *The Glory Years.* San Diego: Union-Tribune Publishing Company, 1964.

WHEN SAN DIEGO WENT DRY

San Diego Sun. June-July, 1919

San Diego Union. June-July 1919

THE TUMOR MANIA

San Diego County, Superior Court. "People vs. Mrs. Lou Patterson." Case no. 345. Research Archives, San Diego Historical Society.

San Diego Union. 22 July 1882.

San Francisco *Chronicle.* 28 July 1882.

THE LAST OF THE *NARWHAL*

San Diego Union. 12-13 February 1932, 31 October 1932, 24 November 1933, 24 August 1937.

Index